RESTORED

GOD'S NOT DONE WITH YOU

Josilyne Thomas

DEDICATION

This book is dedicated to my husband Kenny Thank you baby for always pouring into me, for pushing me, and for helping me to write this book.

I want you to know I am grateful for how you love me as Christ loved the church. Because of you, I was able to love again! You inspire me to be everything God has ordained me to be. To my arrows, Aliyana, Kaleb, Javion, Kristian, and my furbaby Karter; mommy loves you all unconditionally. I am honored God chose me to steward over you!

PREFACE

In life, we all face some sort of hardship, dark seasons, or pressing. Those things are not meant to break us. In fact, those seasons come to mold us, shape us, grow us, develop us, and prepare us for who we were created to be. After all, every diamond must go through a high-pressure environment. That is very much like our lives from my point of view no matter what hardships you have faced in life. I have learned that being transparent, authentic, and vulnerable has allowed others to see that I was once lost, but now I'm found.

I believe that each and every one of us has the capability to grow, and transform into whom God has called us to be. Many of us are not who we used to be five years ago. Ten years ago. Or even twenty years ago. Praise God! In this journey of our lives and figuring out our purpose here on earth, we are being pruned, pressed, and pricked, which allows room for the transformation process to begin, but it requires us to have a sensitive ear to hear and a softened heart to be submissive to the journey God's way and not our way.

Proverbs 19:21 Many are the plans in a person's heart, but it is the Lord's purpose that prevails.

FOREWORD

We live in a broken world full of broken people that are striving each and every day to be known, seen, and loved. Many would dare to do almost anything in their power to attain all three.

Many fail to realize that we are human beings created in the image of our creator, God the Father, God the Son, and God the Holy Spirit. We are Image Bearers created in the righteousness of God in Christ Jesus. In all three we are sealed and complete.

Nothing missing, nothing lacking. But why do we fail to realize this? Here's why: until you begin to accept and embrace your true identity in Him, you are bound to the vicious cycle of being known, seen, and loved all by your own free will, might, and strength.

The problem with this dilemma is that when this is done solely in our own strength it leads to much exhaustion, pain, and suffering.

If you (and/or someone you know) can relate to the dilemma described above or desires to know where your true identity comes from, allow this precious book you're holding in your hands, to serve you as an encouragement and reminder of the redemptive power of Jesus Christ!

When we position ourselves to be fully surrendered in Him there is much transformation and restoration. Friend, be encouraged in knowing that God's not done with you.

He will restore every aspect of your life if you allow Him to. Friend, let **Psalm 51:12 (AMP)** be your heart's cry: Restore to me the joy of Your salvation, And sustain me with a willing Spirit.

Carmen Alicea Friend, Sister in Christ, & Mentor

INTRODUCTION

First and foremost, I give all Glory, honor, and power to The Most-High King Jesus for allowing me to have the privilege and boldness to write this book. I procrastinated on writing this book for about five years. I kept making excuses about why I couldn't write it, why I shouldn't write it, and why I was fearful of writing this book.

The Lord continued to press upon my heart why I had every reason to write this book and not prolong it any further. I didn't really know where to begin. I had many thoughts in my mind about all I needed to share, but I couldn't figure out how to begin. One day I just began writing. I began with chapter 4 and hopped around as the Spirit lead me. This book was not written in order at all.

There were many times I wanted to sugar-coat some of the events that occurred in my life, to protect others, to protect myself. God said, "NO." He has already gone before me. He has written my story way before I was even born. He knew the many mistakes I would make, He knew the traumatic experiences I would face, and He knew how my life would shift for the better. Through it ALL He loved me through it. He has shown me grace, day after day.

Reader, I want to prepare you that many of these real-life experiences may get touchy for you, but they're real, they're my story and I have been Refined, and Restored.

Writing this book was not easy, and it has been a season of healing for me. Many times I entertained the thought of quitting and not finishing this book. It got real again for me. I had to put myself back into the shoes of the old me for a minute to be able to write this as real as God instructed me to.

In writing this book, I have cried, I have been frustrated, the enemy tried to instill shame upon me, and even felt some anger arise. But the Lord continued to remind me that I am not who I used to be, I am not that person once entangled with worldly things. He has forgiven me, He still loves me, He has Refined me, Restored me, Redeemed me, and I get to share this beautiful journey of how Christ transformed my life and encourage you that if He can do it for me, He most certainly can do it for you! Be encouraged. You are loved!

2 Corinthians 3:18 And we all, who with unveiled faces contemplate the Lord's glory, are being transformed into his image with ever-increasing glory, which comes from the Lord, who is the Spirit.

Romans 3:23 For all have sinned and fall sort of the glory of God.

John 8:7 When they kept on questioning him, he straightened up and said to them, "Let any one of you who is without sin be the first to throw a stone at her."

CHAPTER ONE

LA LINDA

I don't remember much from my childhood or pre-teen years. What I do remember are flashes of memories that remain clear in my mind. So bear with me as I try and share as much as I could remember for myself. One thing I clearly remember that my siblings and I laugh all the time about now is when I was about two, we were having fellowship in the cafeteria after a church service and about to head to the nursing home with my family where they served after church. I remember asking my oldest sister if she could take me to the bathroom because after drinking a lot of coffee, I had to go. She said, "no," and told me to go alone. I was scared but I went alone because I had to go so bad. When I came out, it was quiet and dark.

My pants were unbuttoned since I didn't know how to button them and I had coffee and a piece of bread with me. I was on Broadway Street in Camden all alone locked in a church looking out the tiny window that shed a glimpse of light. My parents had forgotten me and didn't notice until they were inside the nursing home and rushed back to get me. That was the first memory of me ever feeling forgotten about but hasn't been the last.

LESSONS I LEARNED:

- **Many times in life we may feel abandoned by God. Have you ever been there? Physically we feel forgotten, but the reality is, sometimes God puts us in tests early in life to strengthen us, not to weaken us. In order to do His will, we must be strong. The next time you feel left out or abandoned I want you to remember this, "Eli, Eli Lama sachthani?" Jesus cried out My God, My God, Why have you forsaken me? In Matthew 27:46 But the reality is, that God never left, He is always in us as we are in Him. Just because you don't feel His presence doesn't mean His presence is not there.**

I remember that since I was about two years old I was raised by my step-father along with my mother. To me, he wasn't my step-father because I never knew him like that, I only knew him as my Papi (daddy). In other words, He was my dad, the man who raised me, the only man I knew. I don't know much about my biological parents' story. I only know some things because it's what I was told growing up. I was told my parents split up because my father was an alcoholic which triggered him to be very physically abusive to my mother. I know he did time in prison, I don't know for what but I know he would send us birthday cards, and draw us colored pictures on small pieces of handkerchiefs. My mother eventually fought for full custody of us and she won that case. I remember occasionally my biological dad coming to visit us. I was my parents' youngest child. I have two older sisters and a brother. Later in life, my mother adopted three other children and had custody of three others who eventually went back with their mom. They were all family-related to us. My mother raised ten kids. So you could imagine how loud, crazy, busy, and dramatic our home always was, but I wouldn't want it any other way.

I remember at one of our family parties my mother told me to go sit with my dad and I went to sit with my dad. Little did I know my biological father was also at this party and he was expecting me to go sit with him, but I didn't know any better and he was not very happy that I sat with the one I knew as my dad. The older I get I become more and more curious as to what my biological father was like. What did he like? What did he like to do besides drink? What was his favorite color? Favorite car? Favorite hobby? Did he play any sports in school growing up? What is his side of the story about my parent's relationship? I have so many questions that I will never get the opportunity to know from him, but only through the lens of other people who knew him.

Growing up, I didn't have much interest in getting to know him or even paid much attention to when he came, not on purpose, but I was in my own little bubble. I just did as I was told. As an adult, I find myself thinking of him more and more and hoping I could get one last conversation with him, but I will never get that opportunity and that hurts! When I was about eighteen years old I was told my father wasn't going to make it. He had drunk so much that he ruined his liver. He was told if he stopped drinking he would be on the list for a liver transplant to save his life. But he didn't stop, and sadly, he passed away. My siblings spent my dad's last days and hours with him in the hospital room. It was hard, having to run back and forth to the hospital not knowing when was the moment he would take his last breath. I remember holding his hand and him not being awake but hearing my voice and squeezing my hand to let me know he knew that I was there. I whispered to him that I was pregnant with my first child, but I'll get into that later. I just wanted him to know because I knew he wouldn't get the opportunity to meet my daughter. We spent his last moments with him and it was rough, but I was also happy to be able to at least be there with him.

Out of all my siblings, I was the one who looked identical to my father. He was light-skinned with blonde hair. I was the lightest one of my siblings and the only one with dirty-blonde hair. My dad's nickname was Pucho, so they nicknamed me Puchita because they said I was his twin. I HATED IT! I would cry because I hated to hear them say that I looked just like my dad. In my mind what I knew about him and all I knew was that he loved to drink, he hurt my mom, and with that came hurting us, because we didn't get to see him or spend time with him, so that made me angry. I would roll my eyes or get angry when they would call me Puchita. As I ponder, I'm just curious to know why my father drank so much. Was he hurting? Was he trying to mask something that he felt he couldn't deal with? Was he broken and felt that alcohol was the only thing that numbed what he needed at the moment? Did anyone care to ask or help him? Knowing that he was an alcoholic and it ruined his life, has allowed me to want to stay far away from it, and to me, it didn't taste good anyway. As an adult, I am more accepting of the fact that I look just like my father and I'm okay with that. When my dad came to visit us he would always say, "La Linda". Which means beautiful, or pretty in Spanish. So in honor of him, and to remember that saying I got a tattoo of that phrase.

LESSONS I LEARNED:

- **There is a commandment in the bible that says, Honor thy mother and thy father. It's the only commandment that comes with a promise from God, that we will live a long life. When my biological father was on his death bed as I was holding his hand, I would dare say I had**

legit reasons to be angry. But the bible does not say Honor thy mother and thy father whether they deserve it or not. It just says to honor them. No matter their wrong-doings, they played a role in us being here on earth. We can either choose to love or choose to hate. It's easier to hate than it is to love. The reality is, that nothing in life is easy, not even forgiving the ones who hurt you. Your level of forgiveness will show your level of character.

I am a daddy's girl. I adore my step-father, (to be clear I never called him or labeled him my step-father and I still don't because he IS my father, I'm only putting it that way so you know who I'm talking about.) I was his shadow growing up. Wherever you saw my Papi, you saw me. He raised us to be amazing kids. We weren't always perfect and I'm sure at times rough to deal with but he had so much patience with us. He was the best thing that happened to my mother and I am so grateful that we had and still have the opportunity to have him in our lives to raise us and guide us along the way. He was the one who took my siblings and me to school in the mornings. He taught us the importance of being on time everywhere we had to go. He is an amazing chef and I learned to cook from him. He taught me to drive, took me to get my license, and took me to buy my first car ensuring that the money I saved would be put to good use.

Most of my life lessons and what helped shape me into the hard worker and go-getter I am today are because of him. I'm sure there were many opportunities where he could have said, "forget this I'm out, these aren't my biological kids," yet he stayed. He showed loyalty, love, and consistency. He showed that commitment wasn't always feeling like it, but still stayed because he was committed. If I had an issue or something heavy that I needed advice about, he was the first person I would run to. He showed us what a real man was and what we should expect our future husbands to be. A god-fearing man who taught us the ways of the Lord and taught us what it was to walk according to God's word and God's ways. I remember as a child we had weekly bible studies in our living room. My dad would teach us the word of God and have us read it for ourselves. Back then we had no clue what we were reading but today we are seeing the Bible come to life in things my dad taught us when we were young. The imprint left on our little hearts as young children that we could still think back and remember that our foundation built on God was taught way long ago.

My mother was one of the strongest women I have ever met. I love my mother deeply. She has always done her best to provide for us and to make sure we lived a pretty decent life. My mother will forever be one of the strongest women I have ever met in my life. One that shows that no matter what she has been through in life she continues to persevere. Hearing the horrific stories about the abuse from my biological dad and seeing how my mother overcame those dark seasons in her life is admirable. My mother was tough. She is tough! I wouldn't blame her though. She was tough because she probably felt she had to be after dealing with so much abuse and heartaches. She was protective. She had walls up. She loved her children hard and would do anything for us, but sometimes I felt that she was so tough that sometimes she forgot to nurture us.

I wanted to feel more loved by my mom. Not that she didn't love us because I know she did, I just wished I felt it more. My dad told us he loved us, but he also showed us. I totally get it, she has been through a lot. Growing up in our household was rough, but I'm sure it could have been worse. Although our parents showed us consistency and were molding us to ensure we were great adults, it was tough. I felt very isolated from many things growing up. My mother tried to protect us, but in my opinion, it became sort of a way to control us. Protecting us is different than controlling us.

I didn't feel like I had much opportunity to figure out who I really was as a young kid. I don't feel I was able to explore different options. So when I did get the opportunity to be, "free," I kinda, sorta went a little overboard. I wished that as a child my mother would have sat and had conversations with us about consequences that would occur if we did certain things, not just threatened us with consequences about things she didn't want us to do. That only put fear in us and made us want to go out and explore those things. That's like telling a child not to touch the stove because they'll get burned, what do you think they're going to want to do? Touch the stove. It's called curiosity.

In school, I wanted to be on a team and try different sports. I asked my parents if I could be a cheerleader, run track, play basketball, do gymnastics, dance, play an instrument, and much more. I didn't get an opportunity to do any of the things I asked to try. I was able to try the recorder which every kid in school got to try. At about twelve years old I took art lessons in church, which I loved, and had the best instructor ever. That's about it. Which explains why now as an adult I learn so many different creative things. I never want to stop learning and growing because I am now exploring what I never got to explore as a kid. I had a wild imagination and I still do, which is great that I never lost that with age. I still remain a dreamer.

We visited our family often in Massachusetts and we loved going. I had always loved seeing my cousins and aunts from there. We would always play cops and robbers, tag, hide-n-seek, basketball, and much more. I remember being about seven or eight years old and hiding in one of the beds in my cousin's room. While everyone ran around chasing each other and trying to find whoever was missing. One of my male cousins saw me in the bed and jumped on top of me and started humping me with my clothes on. I panicked, I had no clue what he was trying to do or what that meant, but I froze in fear because I knew one thing for sure that wasn't normal. Someone was about to come in and he hopped off the bed and continued to act like we were all playing. I didn't think much of it and I didn't say anything to anyone until I shared it with my sisters when I was about twenty-four years old. I'm grateful for whoever that was that popped through that door because that could have ended a different way. No matter how much I have tried to erase that moment, I can't. I just learned to stay in close proximity to my parents and/or my sisters for protection and stay away from him!

I remember moving around New Jersey very often as a young kid. It seemed like every time we settled in a home and got comfortable it was time to move again. I hated moving around so much. I hated packing and unpacking. Having to move lots of heavy furniture over and over again. I needed stability. We needed stability. I also don't have all the answers as to why my parents needed to move us multiple times, but I'm sure they had a good reason to do so. We just learned to adjust and deal with it.

We struggled a lot growing up. I remember having our lights shut off many times. We would even see my father get creative and cook meals that weren't ideal for a meal, but fed us. I remember seeing him make food and use the kerosene heater with a pan to cook because our stove wasn't working due to no electricity. We used any candle we found in the home as a source of light. Having to wash our laundry in our bathtubs or sink. Use a sock or a cut-up shirt to wipe ourselves when using the restroom. Many times we used detergent to wash the dishes or shampoo to wash our bodies. One time we had to go stay with our grandmother because where it was freezing cold as young kids. We had a dog, but my grandmother didn't want our dog at her house, so we had to leave her behind.

When my parents went to check on her the next morning, she was dead because of how cold it was. It was a sad time for us. I even recall as a teenager having to live in a motel with my family. Almost ten of us were in a one-bedroom motel. Two beds, one couch, and one shower, and we would just lay wherever we could find a spot to rest before we had to go to school the next day. Talk about humble times. Talk about the struggle. Talk about a dark season. My God. It didn't matter what we hoped we had that we didn't have. What matters is what we did have, and how hard my parents worked to do the best they could with what they had. One thing is for sure, they always made sure we had God in our hearts, clothes on our backs, food in our bellies, and some kind of roof over our heads.

As far as I could remember I started going to church as a Lutheran with my parents in Camden, NJ. Then when I was about six or seven I remember going to a Christian church and that's how we began to learn about Christianity and what being a Christ-follower meant. Although I didn't understand everything at such a young age, I knew that God was real because I witnessed many miracles happen just before my eyes.

Lessons I learned:

To be grateful for anything we have, even if it's not everything we want.

CHAPTER TWO

GIRL, YOU'RE PUSHIN' IT

The teenage years are supposed to be some of your best years. The years when you begin to find out who you are, to develop relationships with individuals outside your home, the years when you are sort of becoming your own person. My teenage years are also remembered in flashes, but I remember more from these years. Some things I am glad I remember and some that I wish I could have forgotten. I recall a point in my early adolescent years when I felt like I didn't belong. I felt like I was ignored, pushed to the side, and I wasn't able to really live life or enjoy it. I felt trapped in this cocoon that for whatever reason just wouldn't crack open. I began having suicidal thoughts without even really knowing much about it or how to be successful, or even what God had to say about it. At that point, I didn't realize that God never wastes the pain we endure in this life. He uses it for good and will use it to help others that are struggling, but I was too young to realize that.

I had a thick, black, leather belt and used it to strangle myself in my room. I choked, turned red, coughed, felt intense pressure on my face, and felt my eyes bulging, yet I was still there. My mother walked in on me doing that and snatched the belt from me and questioned why I was attempting to do such a thing. I could barely utter a word. But inside I was screaming for help that at that moment I feel like I didn't receive. I hated life and questioned my existence. As I shared in the previous chapter, I wanted to enjoy life and be a part of something I feel like I was never able to be a part of. In school, I wanted to play sports, run track, be in a play, play an instrument, be a cheerleader, something. I WANTED TO DO SOMETHING! I wanted to figure out what I liked and what I disliked, just like a normal teenager, but the only thing I disliked was being THERE!

In my adolescent to teen years, I was always the tomboyish type of girl because I was close in age to my brother and I was always hanging out with his friends. Which I loved because there was always less drama. Football, basketball, dodgeball, tag, and playing cops and robbers were the kinds of things we liked to play growing up. The majority of the time I was the only girl unless my best friend at the time would come by and she would be right alongside us. I loved hanging out with her because back then, to me, we resembled one another in looks and in how we just loved being athletic. She was funny, witty, athletic, and tough. She had a brother and we all knew one another, we grew up together because we attended the same church and school. Also, our parents knew one another from high school. Our brothers were very close and she and I were practically inseparable. We had known one another since about the age of eight and her brother and I liked each other, but we were only eight!!!! By the time we were in sixth grade, we expressed to one another that we liked each other. I would say that was around the time that I began being interested in boys and actually finding them attractive and not considering them just my homie.

We started talking, like more than friends, whatever that meant in sixth grade. While in school, we would walk each other to class, flirt, write notes and give each other, "love taps." You know, the things sixth graders would do when they were, "in love." One day my mother found out and she waited until I got home from school, but before I could even explain anything or tell her what I was feeling or defend my case she was yelling and screaming and threatening me with what would happen if I didn't stop talking to him. I really didn't do anything wrong at that time, I hadn't even kissed him at that time, but that was the beginning of me feeling like I couldn't share anything opposite-sex-related with my parents because they didn't want to hear anything at all about it. It was their way or no way. So I lived my life internally which caused me to feel like I didn't have a voice to share or express those things that I had to bottle up day after day. I became the person who just held everything in, not wanting to share much with anyone. Especially my parents.

My mother's threats didn't make me stop liking him, he hadn't done anything wrong to anyone for them NOT to like him. We were young, I get it now, but controlling someone doesn't make them submit to your authority. In reality, her threatening me just forced me to put walls up and pushed me to be secretive. He and I really liked each other and were steady dating in sixth grade, but he had moments when he wanted to flirt with other people as well. But to us, dating meant seeing eachingther at school, at church, writing love notes, flirting at lunch, kissing a few times, and telling all our friends we were together.

One summer for our church we went on a youth camping trip away from home. We had been on and off for a couple of years now and during our camping trip we had been "on." We were excited to be at camp together and just be able to spend time together that weekend and hang out. We had a great few days and I was fulfilled because camp in its totality was the best time I ever had. Besides the moment that I almost drowned in five feet of water, while I went down a slide at what felt like as fast as 50 miles per hour knowing I can't swim, thankfully, my friend saved me. While another time that weekend I thought I was drowning in the lake while I was in a canoe that flipped over and all I had to do was stand up in the shallow water. We all laughed and still laugh to this day.

On our way home from camp we were all exhausted and worn out. The buses were loaded with tired and depleted youth, exhausted youth group leaders, and a youth pastor who I'm sure was just happy the weekend was ending and he managed to keep every one of us alive and safe. I thought everyone on the bus was sleeping, but that was until I heard our youth pastor yelling at someone telling them to get to the back of the bus. As we looked up I saw my "boyfriend" and sister getting yelled at and they were being separated. We had the most confusing look on our faces and wondered what had happened. After a few moments had passed, we found out that they were getting in trouble because they were caught locking lips. Yep, you got it. My boyfriend was caught kissing my sister. Oh, the rage I had felt, and the betrayal I had experienced at that moment. How could he? How could SHE?!

The remainder of the ride back home was so quiet you could hear a pin drop on that bus. I felt like all eyes were staring at me because everyone knew about him and me, which made things much more awkward. He is the first boy I loved, the first boy I really cared about, and to know that I had just been betrayed by the both of them was beside me. Upon our arrival, my parents were informed about what my sisters doing and the family car ride back home seemed even more awkward. She got yelled at and was in trouble, and I sat in silence trying to gather my thoughts on how I could convince my parents that the boy that I raved so much about being with, just kissed my sister, but he really liked me. How stupid did I really look or sound to my parents? We got home and my sister wanted to talk. I listened to her apology and how she claims that she didn't mean for it to happen, but it just accidentally happened?

Do you mean to tell me, both of y'all lips just accidentally locked and there was no self-control from either one of you? That is so hard to believe and at that moment I was so enraged. I shared with her how I really felt about it all and couldn't share another word with her for many days after that. I was crushed. I was angry. I was confused. I wanted to explode. But with time, she and I moved past it and I dealt with him differently, but that didn't last too long.

I had broken up with him for a little bit and eventually, he sucked me right back into being with him years later. Haven't I learned my lesson already? Apparently not! His apologies, his sorry's, and his pleading for us to be together again seemed sincere, so I said yes and forgave him. We were on this journey of figuring it all out and really telling one another we wanted to be together. We were in high school at this point and I thought things were better. That is until I found out from a classmate that the boy that I have forgiven time after time after time, and been with off and on for years had gotten some girl in our school pregnant!

You're with me, dating me, yet you got some other girl pregnant? We were young and I was naive to think if he cheated on me with a family member why would it be any different? This time around though that was it for me. I began realizing that the me he claimed he wanted to be with was just NOT enough for him and he proved that to me many times. So this time I decided no matter how hurt and crushed I was, I had to part ways with him. Was it easy? No.....very difficult, but I could not keep doing that to myself, so I let her deal with the person that I knew he would continue being, and he did. Many years later, as adults, we saw one another and he gave a few hints that he was still interested in me, I was happily taken and I knew that entertaining that thought wasn't even an option for me.

It was sweet at sixteen, but not for long. I had it in my mind that as long as you make it to the age of sixteen being a virgin that two things would happen. First, you would have a huge sweet sixteen birthday party with the beautiful fancy gown with all the girls in your court wearing fancy, cute dresses. Second, you would be honored and praised for saving yourself and being pure at sixteen. To me that was huge. I was always threatened that I better not have sex before marriage, or else. I never had a real honest one-to-one with my mom about why I really shouldn't have sex before marriage and what God expects from us in that area. All I knew is that I was sixteen and hadn't had sex and to me that was honorable. I wasn't recognized and to me being recognized meant you got a sweet sixteen party. Well, that didn't happen. I got a cake, and balloons, and had a few friends over at the house for my sixteenth birthday. I was confused, what happened to honoring my purity? Since that was not done, I didn't care anymore about remaining pure. I felt like I did my part, I remained pure until I was sixteen. I did it my way, not God's way.

At the time where we lived there was a guy who went to school with my sisters and he that had just bought a house down the street from us with his girlfriend at the time. He lived so close that we could see his house from our front porch. I didn't meet him as our neighbor though, I met him when I was ringing up his groceries as a cashier down the street from where we lived at just fifteen years old. He flirted with me, but it wasn't anything big at that time. He became very close with my family, he was one of my brother's close friends, and my parents eventually grew to love him and accept him into our home.

During that time we struggled a lot as a family. There were moments when my parents didn't have money to buy food, or pay for all our bills and they were very transparent with him about that. He was so kind and genuine, had a selfless heart, and any time he could, he was there helping my family. I remember many times he knew we were struggling, he would order pizza and had it delivered to our home asking for nothing in return. He and I grew a bond because he was around often, and I could see how compassionate, tender, and kind he was. He seemed to be drawn to me, and I was drawn to him as well. I was sixteen and he was twenty-one. That clearly didn't matter. Our interests in one another became more than just a little crush. Being that he was years older than I was, had a car, a house, and seemed to have his life together, it fascinated my sixteen-year-old little self.

He was over our house a lot. The more he was over, the more I liked him, and the more I could see that he liked me too. The porch was the "hangout spot." When our company came over we always enjoyed being on the porch. Many times he would be on the porch alone with me. He began giving me signals that he wanted to be more than just my neighbor. More than my sister's classmate. More than my brother's friend and I liked it.

He became very flirtatious and I didn't stay too far behind. He began driving my brother and me to school because he would see us walking down the street passed his house to go to our bus stop and I'm sure it was his agenda to get closer to me. IT WORKED! Those car rides in his Lexus would always have a fresh red rose in the front seat waiting for me and it was a sweet gesture that made my day. I felt special. I'm not sure if those were pulled daily from his garden or if he bought them daily, but that was the least of my concerns. The drop-offs at school suddenly became pick-ups during school, except they weren't when the school day was over. I started cutting school and leaving early to be with him. I wasn't failing in school, all my work was always turned in, but leaving to go be with him and my parents not knowing for a long time seemed like the best thing in MY world at that time.

Our porch visits suddenly became a place where we secretly began showing affection to one another. Any moment we were left alone even for a second he would quickly kiss me, hug me, and even touched me intimately. We would kiss and touch quickly, hoping someone wouldn't peek out the window or open the front door and catch us. I knew it was not ideal because of the age difference, and because he had a girlfriend, but I liked how he made me feel, so my morals went out the door. A few weeks after he and I started to pursue whatever it was we had together, he told me he had gotten married to his girlfriend. I was devastated and wondered why would he lead me on if he knew he wanted to be with her forever and had planned on marrying her. He gave me a bunch of excuses for not walking away at that point because I was already invested. I had feelings. I was a sixteen-year-old, with feelings and I didn't know how to control them. So walking away from someone who I admired after time was invested after I felt something

I never felt before was almost impossible. So, I kept going.

Time had passed and my parents had still not found out about him and me. My brother was the only one that knew what we had been feeling for one another, but he stayed out of it. One day he picked me up from school along with my cousins and my best friend at the time. We all hung out at my cousin's house when we should have been at school. He and I decided to leave the group and go to my cousins' room and "hang out" in private. I can picture the day and what I was wearing as if it were yesterday. We had no intentions of doing anything other than talk and make out. Well, at least I didn't have any intentions.

But that quickly changed. We began kissing, it became more passionate. More than usual since we were alone and in private and we didn't have to quickly sneak a kiss as we did on the porch back at home. I started to feel flutters in my stomach and things started happening to my body. Things that I have never felt before. As I pulled him in closer, I could feel my body telling me one thing and the little girl in me felt another.

I was nervous but felt ready. As I whispered to him I told him I was ready. He questioned, "Ready for what?" I said, "You know, to do IT". He kept asking me if I was sure because he didn't want me to regret it later. It was a huge step and decision for me to make since I was a virgin. He told me he didn't want me to regret anything. I continued to tell him that I was sure and that I knew I wanted to continue. Then it happened!!!! Afterward, it was a bit awkward. Here I am lying naked next to a man who I just gave myself to.

I barely wanted my mother or sisters to see me naked, so a man seeing me naked was embarrassing. I became fearful. What if my mom noticed me acting funny or walking funny. Then what? I had so many concerns and questions. Most of all I felt like that just drew me closer to him, but in all actuality what it really did was create a soul tie. I not only willingly gave him the most precious and innocent part of my being. I also gave him a piece of my soul. The part of me that I was supposed to save until marriage for the one and only man that God predestined for me.

As time went on, we met anywhere we could and were intimate wherever we could. The more we had sex, the more natural it became and the more comfortable I felt. He began exposing me to several sexual acts and soon enough I thought I became an expert. I knew God wasn't pleased. I knew my parents would not be pleased. But somehow I managed to get through the uncomfortable moments and enjoy the sin that to me was pleasurable, but for a moment. He would sneak me into his home through the garage during the broad daylight when I was supposed to be at school.

One day my father came to his house while I was there and I had to hide in one of the bedrooms scared to death that my father would say that he knew I was there and he came to get me. Another time, I got off of work early and instead of calling my dad to pick me up, I decided to call him. He picked me up and we went driving around for hours just listening to music. When we pulled up at my job, there was my dad waiting for me. He was so angry and I was terrified. My mom made me quit that job after that and I was angry at myself, but mostly for getting caught.

I still was attending school and sooner than later my mother began to notice that I was tucked away in my room more often. She came up to check on me one evening and there I was writing him a "love letter". It had TMI (too much information) in this letter that I planned for my brother to give him. She found out I was cutting school to be with him, I loved him and we had been messing around for a long time. In that letter luckily I didn't write anything about us being intimate, but I'm sure my mom assumed by what was written in that letter and the feelings expressed to him. She and my father had decided to make a hard decision and pull me out of school. I was a junior and about seventeen by this time.

She wanted to know if I was a virgin or not so she took me to a doctor's office, and had them check me to see if they could determine if I was a virgin, or not. I felt so uncomfortable and awkward. Not to mention very embarrassed. The doctor told my mom they could not determine or decide if I was or not. And I was so afraid to speak to my mom about regular everyday life stuff, so how could I possibly open up and tell her I was sexually active. My mom was so angry that she told me if she found out that I was not a virgin that she would call the police and get him locked up because I was a minor and he was an adult. They were done with him, and probably me too. I was terrified mostly because I was scared she would get him locked up.

Here I was, one year away from graduating. I was on lockdown in my home. I couldn't go anywhere with anyone unless it was with my parents. If I thought I was in prison living there, it just became one hundred times worse. I had no job because my parents made me quit, I graduated a year late, and I barely got to see people, unless it was right next to my parents. I remember being called a "whore" because my mother found sexy underwear in my dresser and found out I was grooming my private parts.

My mother had no filter in saying what she felt and how she felt it. He suddenly became my parent's worse enemy and I guess all that he ever had done for my family in regards to helping with food, bills, and money was just forgotten about. They despised him, and at that moment I hated them for isolating me from the world and degrading me for my mistakes rather than making it a teachable moment and displaying love and forgiveness.

My brother and I were very close during these years. He had a prepaid phone and would let me use it often to allow me to secretly call him because he knew I was suffering and struggling silently. I would write letters and he would be the messenger back and forth between us. There was a time when I was just tired of it all so I ran away to my best friend's house. I felt angry and felt like I was going to explode because I was being punished and none of it seemed fair to me. He was free and living his best life, married, with a kid, yet there I was carrying the weight of both of our mistakes all alone. He would pass by our house with his car system blasting to "Song Cry" by Jay-Z because he knew that was a song we always listened to together and he told me that when he would drive by blasting it, it was to let me know he was thinking of me. He did it often and it brought me joy and an ounce of hope that when my prison sentence was over, somehow, someway we would be together. I guess that was the little dreamer in me. Hoping it would all work out how I imagined and envisioned it in my mind. I really hoped that we would work out and make it because I gave him my virginity. To me, that was sentimental and of great value, therefore, the thought of not being with him forever scarred me.

I gave him the purest, most precious part of me and thought that if I kept giving myself to him he would choose me and wait for me, but it was only a fantasy.

After my mom pulled me out of school I told my best friend at the time what happened. She and I were so close, we were inseparable, she knew EVERYTHING about him and me. Weeks later I saw my cousin at seven eleven and I asked her if what I was hearing was true about my best friend and the guy I was dealing with. She looked at me puzzled and said she didn't know anything and I knew deep inside she was covering up for my best friend, who was also her mutual friend as well. It hurt because as much as I understand how close we all were, we are family. But that just gave me a different perspective about family. Not everyone that is your family looks out for you and there are friends that are closer to you than family. I asked her over and over to tell me, and she didn't, but her reaction said it all.

Time went by and I wrote a letter asking him if he was dealing with her behind my back while my mom had me on lockdown. There were so many lies going around back and forth just so I didn't find out. I loved him and the last thing I wanted to hear was that he was messing with my best friend. He eventually came clean about it. He told me that he had slept with her one time, and it was an accident.

I was so furious, heartbroken, and angry and I wanted to fight. I couldn't believe what I was hearing. I gave myself to him and got caught and was on lockdown, not able to graduate with the official class I was set to graduate with because I was dealing with him, and he betrays me this way? I was betrayed not just by a man who claims he loved me so much and wanted to be with me, but by my very own best friend. Someone who knew everything about me, who I called my sister. That's why you have to be careful with those who are in your circle. Not everyone is really for you. Some come to gain information to then use it against you for their advantage. At sixteen I wasn't wise enough. I told her everything about him and me, which is what made her probably want to take her chance and be with him. I messed up. I learned my lesson not to tell the most intimate things to people.

For weeks and months, I didn't talk to any of them. My heart was bleeding and there weren't enough bandages that could stop it at that point in time. After time went by, he and I spoke and he apologized. I honestly didn't know if it was sincere because they continued being together. It wasn't just a one-time thing. He went from me, then to her and I was left unpure, aching and feeling robbed. Anything he has asked me to do I did for him, sexually. Why wouldn't he wait for me? Why did he feel the need to sleep with my best friend and continue to do so? Was I not good enough? Was she what he wanted all along? Was he what SHE wanted all along? At what point did they begin to even like one another? I had a million questions that I felt most were left unanswered. I had to move on.

I couldn't wait and hope that he would leave her and we would be back together after I was off of lockdown. Because even if he did, he was still married. My world was in a whirlwind of many different emotions and I was very young and unwise to even begin to try and process it all. I had no one to talk to. I just know I felt robbed. In 2013, I had a dream about her and reached out via social media. We spoke for a little and she apologized after I was able to share and express my feelings toward her. It was hard but I know forgiveness is key to healing from past hurts and wounds. As for him, he and I spoke in person and he apologized. I accepted it and forgave him. There's nothing like trying to forgive someone who you cared for deeply and who betrayed you, but forgiveness is more for me than for the other person. I needed to be able to move past it regardless of the pain and the hurt I felt.

What I wish I knew about purity: The blood-filled vessel is a sign of a covenant between the bearer and whoever plunges into her opening. Sex is a fun-filled activity but breaking the virginity is not a casual act of fun. It is rather a serious covenant struck by the bloodshed on that day. And I believe this is God's way of highlighting that sex is ordained for the husband and wife who have agreed to live together for life. The reason sex was designed by God after the marriage contract is sealed is for fun, procreation, and the purpose of their bond. There exist a spiritual bonding and a sacred process that takes place the very moment the tissue breaks. Basically, there is the essence of blood in every covenant and this is why the membrane contains enough of it. Hence, there is the bathing of the man with her blood to initiate a covenant that is highly recognized spiritually, emotionally, and physically.

To my dear ladies, a bit of your virtue leaves you each time a man enters into you and when that man leaves you. The big question here is how much of yourself has left you? Imagine your virtues that would be lost each time a man enters you without any properly signed marriage bond. The fun part of pre-marital sex is not really funny. That's the irony. What happens in between the lines could be deadly and dangerous. If you give it to your spouse, you lose nothing because he remains with you forever. In that light, he would retain your virtues and never leave with them! Do not open up for one who will carry your worth away or go and dump it in another woman's soul. I hereby boldly say it is an honor to remain a virgin and to experience sex for the first time after your marriage ceremony! I, therefore, urge you to hold your head up and Don't break that gate till marriage. If that gate must break, If your blood in it must be shed, let it be on the body of the man who has married you. At first, virginity was held in high esteem but our generation seems not to treat virginity with its deserved veneration.

Source:
(https://www.modernghana.com/news/929538/virginity-is-the-hymen-enough-covenant.html)

HERE'S THE LESSON:

I hope that the person or people that may have hurt you or betrayed you that are coming to your mind even now you will be able to forgive. Forgiveness is more for you than for them. If you have not forgiven them, they still have control over you. Release that anger, bitterness, and unforgiveness, and be free today FOR YOU! The bible tells us in Matthew 6:14 *that if we forgive other people when they sin against us, our Heavenly Father will also forgive us. He tells us to bear with one another and forgive one another if we have any grievance against someone.* I'm not perfect and I make mistakes daily.

I know I'm in need of forgiveness from others and most importantly God. Therefore, I must forgive others, to get it in return. I challenge you, to forgive others and be free from resenting those who may have betrayed you. Unforgiveness does nothing but keep you bound. BE FREE! In Jesus' name.

CHAPTER THREE

LUKEWARM AT 24

Seven years passed and I didn't recognize the woman I was before those seven years. I had become a mother to what felt like three children instead of two. I had been with the father of my kids in hopes that we could build together and create a life any child, especially mine, deserved. We were high school sweethearts, he was sixteen and I was seventeen years old when we began dating. What caught my eye about him was that he was in great athletic shape, he played football, and he always dressed to impress.

We dated for almost a year, but before we reached that first anniversary I missed my monthly cycle. I was terrified and wasn't sure how I could even face my parents to even explain to them that I was still in high school and potentially on my way to becoming a teen mom. At the time, I lived with my parents and siblings and he lived with his step-father. The plan was that IF I was pregnant I would tell my parents. Preferably my father first, because he was the calm understanding one, and only if my boyfriend's step-father was present with us. I knew how my mother could react and I couldn't bear to even try to imagine raising a child in that type of environment of anger and bitterness because things didn't go as she planned. I wasn't sure how else to take a pregnancy test without my parents finding out so, I walked over to the corner store across the street from where we lived at the time and used their bathroom. I remember my knees shaking heavily as I tried to squat while at the same time trying to urinate on a stick. I held my breath as I waited for the test to determine whether it was a "yes" or a "no". I wondered if becoming a mother against my mother's will would make her hate me. I also wondered if becoming a mother before my time was a huge mistake. But, I also knew that becoming a mother at nineteen would mean having to grow up more rapidly and that although I make mistakes because I am human, God does not make mistakes.

Okay, here we go, the longest five minutes that to me felt more like fifty minutes. I slowly looked down at my pregnancy test while trying to hold my pre-paid cell phone with my hands that felt like jello that I spent minutes on calling my cousin for comfort. "It's a yes!" I cried nervously to my cousin who was anxiously waiting on the other line, as I felt my heart in the pit of my stomach. All I could do was imagine my mother turning into the incredible hulk with the rage she would feel as I shared this news with her. What went through my mind was that she would never allow me to see my boyfriend again, even though he had proven to them that he was a great guy.

A couple of weeks passed and the day came that we would share the news with my parents. I stood on the porch with my boyfriend, and his step-dad, and we called my dad to come out to talk with us. I'm almost positive my mother already had a feeling about what the conversation was about because somehow mothers know everything. We told my dad that I was pregnant and the look on his face was a look of disappointment. He instructed us to go inside and tell my mom the news and as much as I felt like throwing up while walking in the door, I didn't.

I know my facial expressions told my mom everything, so much so that I could have probably saved my breath for another day. After we told her, the reaction we got from her wasn't what I expected, but I believe that's because she already had an idea of what was going on when we called my father outside to talk to him. I knew she was hurt and disappointed, but there was nothing I could do or say to even change anything at that moment.

Fast forward to about four years later. By this time we were living on our own in our very first apartment with our daughter Aliyana for about three years now. Things were okay, but not perfect. Just like any other relationship, we had issues, but we were working on them for the sake of our child and because we thought we were meant to be together. At this time in our lives we had a dog and had taken the dog to the park, but a few weeks before this we found out we were expecting our second child. That day at the dog park changed our lives forever.

Everything seemed fine and normal until I felt extreme pain in my stomach out of the blue and felt my pants get wet. I looked down and we saw a lot of blood. I had no clue what to feel or think at that moment. There were people around, but in those moments of trying to get to the car to get home, then to the emergency room, it felt as though the world stopped and it was just us. I walked into my bathroom and when I pulled my pants down to change, the floor was full of blood and blood clots. I couldn't piece together what exactly was happening, but I could only assume. Shortly after, we arrived at the hospital and it was confirmed that I did have a miscarriage. Not one, but potentially two babies were lost. I was torn apart inside and just sat there with my kid's father feeling like I was shattered into a million pieces. I allowed time for my body to heal, but most importantly my heart. A few months later we began our journey of trying to conceive and a few months later we were blessed with a healthy pregnancy. Our second child Kaleb was born and it just so happened to be the first boy in a long time for our family, the first grandson.

Seven years together, two beautiful children, our son was six months old, and our daughter was five, we were engaged, planning a wedding and lots of couples counseling in preparation for our wedding from a pastor who at the time was a very close family friend ours. From the outside looking in it seemed like we were on the right track and everything seemed to be great, but not everything that glitters is gold. We had a lot of unresolved issues that we just couldn't work past. There were years built up of frustration, broken promises, heartache, anger, lies, and loss of self-worth, I felt unappreciated, devalued disrespect from both sides, and I felt it would be much healthier not to raise our kids in a dysfunctional home.

At that time, I decided it was best if their father and I both went our separate ways so I called off the wedding and we did just that. It was one of the hardest decisions I had to make in my life and also one of the scariest. I knew that if I stayed, my kids didn't deserve the mother they would be getting. They deserved to have me at my best, I was determined to give them that and so much more.

During the time we had been split up my kids' father would come to my apartment to watch our kids because it was easier for us both. At the time I was working full-time during the day, and going to trade school in the evening to be a medical assistant. It worked for us because the kids wouldn't have to get dragged around after school ended they would be home, he would feed them, and get them ready for bed, and for us, it worked. At the time he still wasn't over the fact of us not being together and he began looking through my personal items in hopes to find something. I'm not sure exactly what he was looking to find, and I'm sure he didn't know either, but he did find something.

When I got home one evening after school he asked me why I didn't tell him about a video he found on my small camcorder that I owned. I was never a liar, I never knew how to lie and so my face probably was as if it saw a ghost at that moment. How do I explain this? How come he looked through my closet? What were you searching for? How do I respond? I explained as best as I knew how. The pastor that was counseling us for our marriage, the one that was a longtime family friend, and our pastor at the time had crossed the line. Do you want to talk about church hurt? This is it. There was a time that the pastor called me to speak about our counseling sessions and a conversation that was so innocent quickly turned into me feeling so comfortable that I wanted to crawl out of my skin, vomit, cry, lash out, all the things you could imagine, I felt it. But, I held my composure and just kept silent because I wondered if I told anyone would they believe me? I chuckled a bit so it didn't seem awkward and noticeable, but I knew I had to speak up about this I just didn't know when or how. On that day, I let it be. I stayed silent, not saying a word to anyone.

The very next time I saw his number calling I quickly grabbed my camcorder and recorded what he had shared with me. He stated that he always thought I was beautiful, that he cared about me and loved me in a way more than a pastor should and he knows how wrong that is, he shared how he thought I was very special and near and dear to his heart. He also shared some deeper inappropriate things that I won't repeat, but I got off the phone and was startled. It was extremely inappropriate and I had no clue who to turn to at that very moment because he was such a close friend of my family and they highly respected him. I didn't want to hurt anyone, especially my family so I stayed shut about it and shoved the camcorder in my closet, trying to forget that moment and the one before it. That is until my kid's dad found it.

A part of me did an introspect on myself to see if there was anything I could have done to have made him feel so comfortable to share those things with me. My kid's father questioned me on why didn't I share it with anyone and I explained to him the reasons I just stated. He was furious. He wondered why and how a pastor could be so very blunt about his feelings for someone other than his wife, let alone someone that could be his daughter. He didn't understand how he could counsel us for our marriage yet internally it seemed like he was getting information about us and me while building his agenda secretly. My kid's father always struggled with going to church and building his relationship with the Lord and hearing this just pushed him further away. At the same time, man is not God and no one is or never will be as perfect as God. That does not justify his wrongdoings at all.

My kid's father told me if I didn't tell someone he would. So, I opened up to my father about it first in private because for me it was a touchy and a very uncomfortable situation. My father was hurt because he looked at this man not only as a pastor but also as a close friend and questioned why his daughter. After I shared it with my father the recording, we shared it with my mother and siblings and we were all in tears, and part of us was also enraged. My father reached out to him and told him they had to meet urgently at a park and so they did. My father shared the camcorder recording with him and he didn't deny it at all. He fessed up to his wrongdoings and apologized.

My father told him if he didn't step down from pastoring that he would take the camcorder to the news stations and blast him publicly. He stepped down because he knew it was the right thing to do. My parents had to share with his wife what he had done and I'm sure that was very difficult for them to even do because they loved her dearly. I carried shame for a long time even though there was nothing that I did personally. It took me some time to heal and get over it and for a while, I questioned even stepping foot in another church, and if I did, which one? With time, I trusted the Lord and I was able to move past it.

During that time my kid's dad began dating someone after he accepted the fact that he and I could no longer be together. When I found out he was dating someone I was angry because I didn't want another woman around my kids. I didn't like the thought of them having a stepmother. I was childish and I did childish things to try and get them to split up. I was mean. Plain old mean. I didn't care about anyone's feelings but my own. When I would see her near my kids or at his house when I picked up my kids I would start arguments in the parking lot. I would stand behind her car and call her out hoping to get her sick and tired to the point where she didn't want to even deal with him because of the drama. I was so immature, but I was angry that he was dating someone. Time passed and she didn't leave. They ended up having kids and eventually got married. I still wasn't happy with any of it.

After years passed and she had proven that she was fit and trustworthy for my kids, we began to talk. After many guided conversations, slowly but surely we became closer and closer and have forgiven one another. We have moved passed all the nonsense and childish ways and now have a great relationship and friendship. We love and accept one another's kids as our own and look out for one another. I love her dearly. I love how things are between us now. We watch one another's kids when we need to go out or need a break. It may not always be easy with mending things with your ex's new partner, but it's worth trying and working hard towards it. It has helped us to co-parent our kids much better. It's healthy for all of our kids and us as well. We have determined we are too grown for the drama and it doesn't always need to be drama with raising kids and moving on. I thank God for growing us, making us aware, and mending our broken relationships.

HERE'S THE LESSON:

The Power of the 2nd thought:

Not every decision is the right decision. However, when making a life-changing decision based on emotions and feelings, it would be wise to take a second thought. A wise person will tell you that it's the second thought that matters more than the first thought. Oftentimes, it's our first thought that can lead to hurt, pain, drama, and more. Had I taken second thought at some of my actions, I may not have been in such hurtful situations that upset my family. But on second thought lol maybe this was the path that God wanted me to go down so I could caution those who may be going through it right now.

The Power of Forgiveness:

I had to remember the reasons why it didn't work out with my children's father. It took a lot of healing to get past the fact that another woman was going to be in my kid's life. The only way I was going to get past that is if I started forgiving myself for all the silly things I did on my part. We can't control what other people do, however, we are in charge of what we do. I had to learn my worth for myself and for the sake of my children. Forgiving myself and who I once was and learning about who I am going to become.

Have you forgiven yourself today? Remember no matter how bad the situation is, to have true happiness we must forgive the old self and build with the new self.

I want you to look into the mirror and forgive who you used to be and start building a new relationship with who you are going to become.

CHAPTER FOUR

I FELL IN "LUST"

During the time that my kids' father and I were considering working things out, I was still serving at IHOP. I had become friends with a customer who had become a regular of ours for many years. When we met him he had been single, but during the time that I was working there, he eventually did get married and within a couple of years had a child and his wife was pregnant with their second child. He was about eleven years older than me and only considered him a friend/regular customer. I had spoken to him plenty of times in regards to the situation with my kids' father and me and mentioned that he was looking for work. I realize now that I had given him too much information about my personal life and he used it to his advantage. He knew that I was frustrated with the current relationship I had been trying so hard to work out for my children.

He knew that I was struggling with feeling unappreciated, insecure about my weight after two kids, and struggling with feeling like I was holding down the household with little to no help financially. I felt insecure about my weight because the man I carried kids for and birthed had continuously reminded me that I was heavier than I usually had been in my life and not in a nice way. If that's not enough of an ego killer, I'm not sure what is. So what did that do for me? It left me not only feeling like I was working too much to pay bills but also feeling a void and a sense of feeling unwanted.

The gentleman I was speaking to in regards to this situation had owned his own construction company and offered my kids' father a job. After they had been doing some work together for some time, my kids' father had opened up to him about our relationship as well. What a huge mistake on both of our parts. One day he came to me and told me that my kids' father had tried to get with some girl. I was confused and shocked because in the many years we had been together I have always known him to be one thousand percent faithful. So I was questioning how true this was. I wondered if it was true because of how shaky and unstable our relationship had been at this point. He asked me to meet him so he could prove it to me. He stated that my kids' father said that, the girl had a big butt, and he wanted to get her number. So we met up and he showed me a text that my kids' father had sent him saying that very thing. I felt like my heart had broken into several pieces.

Things were rocky between us, but I was still trying to make things work. But that put the icing on the cake. There were many years of lies, instability, begging him to get work to help me pay bills and care for our children, begging him to stop smoking and lying, broken promises, disrespecting me, not helping me around the house, and much more. I couldn't seem to bare another heartache, so that was it. I was done!!!! I had a conversation with him about the text I saw. He didn't deny it. I questioned internally if that was my customer's motive, to break us apart, although he didn't cause the damage, so he could make a move. But the issue was, I didn't question it soon enough. I was blind, I was vulnerable. I was tender.

And then it began. The plot for my vulnerable, shattered heart to be revived, and I fell for it. I was weak in my mind. What I would give to feel alive, wanted, and secure. I felt bamboozled, but at the time I felt wanted and that's all that mattered in that season. It started as him just hearing me out and giving me advice, but my vulnerability and ignorance led me to fall right into his trap. My morals went right out the window, yet again. Slowly what was only a friendship turned into a relationship. He was tall, attractive, owned his own company, had nice cars, a motorcycle, and a nice home, he was eleven years older than I was, so he had to have it all figured out, right? The problem was, I wasn't the main one. I had become his mistress because I believed what he told me. When he began opening up about how he felt about me, I shared with him that I felt the same way.

But, I knew he was married and I just couldn't do that again, of course, he told me he really didn't love her and that soon they would be divorced anyway. I believed it. We continued. We would meet up whenever and wherever we could just to be able to see one another. Empty parking lots, hotel rooms, in his truck, at my school, at my job, my apartment, and even sometimes at his home. It was a lifetime movie, but it was my reality and I was the star. Deep inside I hated it because I had to share. But another piece of me loved it because of the thrill I got from it also. All I really ever knew was the father of my kids. I never had the space or time to figure out who I truly was. He told me loved me, and with time we became intimate, and he would tell me he wanted to be with me, just "not yet" but soon.

The lies he told me I believed them. He told me, he and his wife didn't sleep in the same room, and I believed it because he would call me at all hours of the night to talk. He would come to visit me at IHOP almost daily. I can still remember his food order as if it were yesterday because that's how much I served him. On my days off, while my kids were in school, he would leave his job sites and come visit me. He became like a drug that I had been addicted to and the more I was with him, the more I wanted him. Because he made me feel "alive!'" During this time I had been attending church and felt like the biggest hypocrite ever. Serving the Lord on Sundays and attending bible study on Wednesdays, yet intentionally sinning on all the other days. I was lukewarm, and deep inside I knew I was wrong and it was unpleasing unto the Lord. Yet, somehow I couldn't stop because my heart was already wrapped up in the fleshly desires that made me feel good. When we first started talking after my breakup I didn't think or plan for it to go this way at all. Things happen, but we also have the free will to choose right from wrong.

I was still living with my kids' dad and his mom during the time we had broken up. My customer would drive by the apartments where we lived at the time and I would either leave with him or follow him to wherever he wanted to meet. This happened for months, countless times. My kids' dad knew and he wasn't happy about it. Eventually, I found my own place because I just couldn't live somewhere with my kids where I felt unwanted and also feeling disrespected when my kids' grandmother put her hands on me. I also needed to live alone so I could have the freedom to do as I pleased.

At the time, I began my journey by going to a technical school to be a medical assistant while serving at IHOP full-time. My son was six months, and my daughter was five years old. On my off days or after work, my customer would come by and see me sometimes quickly and sometimes for long periods. I didn't expect to fall in love with him. Or should I say, in lust with him? He would tell me, "I was different." But what did that mean? All I cared about is that I felt loved and I felt like someone appreciated me. Even if he wasn't mine and even if I knew I was selling myself short. Because in all actuality I knew I was worth more but once I had him, I didn't know how to stop. He taught me things that I never knew before. In a sexual way. Things that I would do just to please him and make him want me even more. It worked! He asked me if we could invite a third person into our sexual relations, just once. I wasn't with it at all. I hated that idea. the thought of it made me internally sick, but I agreed just to try and please him and keep him. But thankfully those plans fell through and it didn't happen.

During that time of this relationship, while attending technical school I had a friend I met there that was going through school with me. A few months passed and I learned that she was dating someone of the same sex. That didn't change my relationship with her although I didn't agree with that lifestyle. I still loved her dearly as a friend and still do. I remember in a conversation we had she told me, "You're gonna like girls also, watch. You're supposed to be with a girl." I told her, "Actually I'm not into that, I know I was born and created to be with a male, and, can't no one tell me any different. That for me was a moment of peer pressure, growing up I knew what the bible said about it and so I didn't dare to even entertain that.

Lesson learned: You can't allow anyone and everyone to speak into you and try to get you to do something you know isn't pleasing to God.

My customer would come over some late nights when the kids would stay with their father, but he could never stay. I would get upset and angry, but who did I think I was? I wasn't his wife. It was as if he took what he needed from me, stayed for a bit after, and left. Yes, I was dumb and naive. Many nights I cried and would be so mad at myself. I would tell myself, "Girl, you deserve better than this, he is playing you, he is not gonna leave his wife." I would call or text him, tell him that and he would suck me back in with his lies and broken promises. I brought up how he claimed he was going to leave her due to his unhappiness, then he told me he couldn't because she was now pregnant with their second child. I wanted to explode. He reasoned that he didn't want to leave her because he didn't want her to get sick and something potentially happen to their baby. So, as a mother myself, I understood and I waited and the vicious cycle continued.

There was a time I had enough and I told him I was done. I just couldn't do it anymore. The pain was too much to endure. I wanted a family. A husband, more kids, a "normal" life. Not one where I was the mistress and someone's sidepiece. So we stopped. My heart felt broken, but it was the right thing to do. I knew I couldn't keep doing this to myself. Weeks had passed between each time I kept telling him this needed to end. Then, he would reach out or I would reach out to him. It was as if I couldn't be with him, but I couldn't be without him either. Or.... I didn't wanna be. There was a point where I tried to work things out with my kids' dad in between one of our "breaks". However, in all honesty, I just couldn't get those feelings back that I once had for him, not only because of all the pain I endured being with him but also because someone else had my full attention and heart. My kids' dad knew my heart wasn't all in it.

He would get upset and curious when I would be in the car blasting the chorus to Usher's song, *"What's a man to do."* Because that song was exactly what I was feeling. "My heart is in two different places, I got you in my life and I wanna do right but it's hard to let it go, when my love has two different faces and I can't break ties cause they both look right." I felt torn in two places, but I knew where I wanted to be at that moment and we both knew it wasn't with him. No matter how hard I tried, I just couldn't. I also didn't want to hurt him knowing I couldn't focus on us fully. My heart belonged somewhere else, even though I couldn't have the full package. I told my kids' dad once again that this wasn't going to work between us. He was a great guy aside from the reasons we broke up but, he just wasn't for me.

During the time that I broke things off with my customer, I had written him an email. In that email, there were so many details about us and things he had said about his and his wife's relationship that I shared with him in that email. Deep, deep things. She even knew that I secretly snuck into his house with his permission as he left the door open while she was home and we spent time together for hours. I was just disrespectful to the max, I was not who I was raised to be. It was as if someone or something had control of me. He got the email and replied, but his wife also viewed that email as well. Things got even more hectic because now she was onto him and every move he made.

From what he shared, they argued, she was angry, he laid low for a bit, but then we started up again. As much as he wanted to be with me, I wanted to be with him. The things that ran through my mind were, '"well if he isn't as happy as he claims and he claims that I'm the one who fulfills that for him, why doesn't he just leave her and things could be more simple." I guess for him things just weren't that simple. During this time, I was late on my cycle and I suspected I was pregnant. When I shared with him that I was late he told me if I was pregnant I couldn't have his child and it would just create more problems for us, in all actuality he meant more for him. I cried and told him I didn't believe in abortions and I would have it no matter what he decided, even if it meant I would never see him again and I would raise the baby alone. A few weeks went by and test after test they kept being negative and I eventually got my cycle. I was relieved and I know he was as well.

My family knew of him and knew that I was dealing with a married man. They weren't happy at all about it. I had the attitude that came off as, I am grown, I take care of myself, and I live by myself, so you can't tell me anything. Yes, I had a point, but at the same time, I should have listened and had more respect for myself. I should have never gotten involved with him, to begin with. Sometimes, we follow our hearts and emotions rather than our heads. Our heart is deceitful and will lie to us. Feelings are fickle, they come and go. I was already too deeply involved and thinking of the pain I would feel just to get out of the situation, I just couldn't imagine, so I dug a deeper hole by continuing to be involved. My family tried to tell me, but I pushed them far away. Many times in life we have to learn the hard way. We have two choices in learning discipline, we do that by either experiencing it or learning it and deciding not to go down that route. That was a time I could have listened, yet I made a choice and had to learn through experience. Hard lessons.

This journey of being his mistress lasted about three and a half years long. We were off and on, but mostly on. There was another time, we decided to break it off. It was a mutual agreement. His wife threatened that if he continued to be with me she would take everything they built together. The kids, the house, the cars, everything. But nothing struck him to his core more than hearing that she would take the kids due to infidelity and she had proof to back it up. Solid proof. He was terrified. He was angry. And for some reason blamed me for her reaction to it all, as if he played no part and I did this all on my own. The audacity of him. I was terrified for myself, for him, and felt bad for her. After he told me what she threatened him with, he told me that if she took his kids he was, "killing everything walking." I told him okay, then we are done. I meant it. After some time had gone by and we weren't seeing one another just texting here and there, I moved on. I was talking to someone else. It was not serious at all, but when he found out we were talking and hanging out, he was FURIOUS! My question to him was how can you be so upset? You are the one who's in a marriage and chose not to leave. He wanted me to stay single because he couldn't have me, but he wanted to stay with his wife as well. Nope! It just doesn't work that way. Slowly, but surely, he came back. He didn't want to leave his wife due to his family but I'm convinced it was because she came from a family that was well off, yet he couldn't stand the fact that I was dealing with someone else. I prayed over and over to God to help me get out of this situation that I got myself into. My specific prayer was, "Lord, please allow something drastic to happen so I wouldn't want to go back to him." As if him having a wife wasn't drastic enough. I believe the Lord heard my prayers and began to intervene because I wanted out! I just knew the pain I would feel in my heart if I did it on my own.

During the three and a half years of us being together, we would help one another out financially if needed. Nothing crazy but if he didn't have it and I did I would help him out and vice versa. But we always paid each other back. It was around tax season and I was always very open with him about everything. I shared with him I had gotten my taxes and he asked me to borrow over $3,500.00 and said he would pay me back slowly. Now, why would someone who owns his own company borrow money from a single mother of two children, going to school and didn't have much herself? I don't know either.

But, I did because I was selfless and giving. He paid me back a few hundred of it weeks after but would not want to speak about the balance that he owed me. Weeks went by, then months, and I began needing this large amount of money for bills. He didn't seem to care. I began getting angry with him ignoring my texts and calls about the money that he promised to pay back. I decided to take all the courage I had within me and go to his house one evening. I was brave! Talk about courage this was it. But I didn't fully think things through either. I grabbed both of my kids and drove to his home. I beeped the horn outside like a mad woman. I saw his son who at the time was about three years of age peek out the window. Seconds later, my heart skipped a beat. I see him yelling and rushing out the front door coming towards my car. I pulled the passenger window down to hear what he was saying and he was yelling, the dialogue went like this:

Him: If you do not get from in front of my house beeping the horn-like you're crazy watch what's gonna happen.

At this time I grab my cell phone and dialed his wife's number, but it went to her voicemail, so she's hearing this voicemail of us arguing back and forth later on.

Me: Well, I'm calling you and texting you for weeks about the money you owe me, the money I need, and no answer.

Him: I said to get from in front of my house, my son is watching and if my wife sees that you're here it's going to be a problem.

Me: All I want is the money you owe me and you will never hear from me again (this time I knew deep inside I had meant it.)

Him: Get away from my house NOW!!!!!!!!

He puts his entire upper body into my passenger window and chokes me as he slams my head into my window. He grabbed my phone from my hands and threw my phone into the graveyard across the street from his house and I knew if I didn't stop and leave that I would probably be there next. I yelled at him to find my phone and I would leave but he just kept screaming for me to leave his house. I turned my car around the dead-end street in his community and began to pull off to try and get away. At this point, both my kids were both crying hysterically because they were terrified. the only thing that ran through my mind was to get away before this man kills me. Mind you, the entire time we were together he NEVER once laid a hand on me, so this terrified me.

But the fear of his wife pulling up from their son's parent/teacher conference and seeing me there would have just put the icing on the cake. I got out of the car to check on my kids and tell them mommy is okay and calm them down. What I didn't know was he was already meeting me across the street and met me face to face with his head. He head-butts me and instantly I felt dizzy as if I was going to blackout and I felt pain in my entire upper face. We are talking about a 6 foot 1 inch male versus a little ole 5 foot 3 inches me. At that moment, I jumped in my car screaming and crying and I saw a father and his son outside of their home in their quiet, very minimal crime community.

I was crying so bad the gentleman couldn't understand what I was saying. I kept looking back hoping that he didn't chase or follow me to finish me off and was grateful to not see him anywhere in sight. I asked this gentleman for his phone to call the police and they instructed me to go straight to the station to put a police report. He asked me who did this and I told him and mentioned I was his mistress. His eyes lit up. I later found out from his wife that not only did she hear my voicemail, but she was embarrassed that I told their friends our business and that they would soon be the talk of the town.

I was able to safely get to the nearest police station and put a domestic violence report in. I remember it clearly. In the police station, almost midnight by this time, both of my kids sitting there shocked, and me even more shocked at what just transpired. The police officer took snapshots of my bruised face and black eye from being head-butt to the face. I asked the Lord for a drastic situation to occur so I can walk away, but I never expected it to be this drastic. He threw my phone and got rid of the only evidence that I had about a large amount of money he owed me which is why I showed up in the first place. And he knew the evidence was on there. I called my sister from the police station and asked her for my cousin's phone number who was probably the only person at the time that I trusted. She asked where I was and why I was calling from a weird number, I said nothing, but the more she interrogated me the weirder I got until I broke down and told her. She said she was coming and I told her please not to call my mother, the next thing I knew, she was there with my mother. We went through months and months of uncomfortable court hearings. He had a lawyer, I of course did not because I couldn't afford one. I pressed charges, put a restraining order, sued him for my money, and gave proof of the statement he made about, "killing everything walking if he lost his family." I disliked court very much but this situation introduced me to court life and I despised it and seeing his face.

I was granted a permanent restraining order, he was ordered to pay some of my money, about $800 of it because that's all I had proof of, he wasn't allowed to come anywhere near my job or my home, and he lost his gun license, and much more, and that was the end of us. His wife contacted me once more during the court hearings, we exchanged words and that was that. I went through many mental battles after that.

HERE'S THE LESSON:

Let's face it, no matter the situation I had gotten myself into knowing the circumstances, it doesn't negate the fact that I'm human and I have feelings. I was blind. I was vulnerable. I was tender. And I found myself there again. Three and a half years were lost from my life because I allowed my fickle feelings to take control of my mind and everything I knew that was wrong. The only thing I got from this relationship were valuable lessons the hard way, abuse, and a love that I experienced that I never had before, but it all seemed like a fairytale.

Many times we have to learn the hard way. That was my hard way. I lost time, friendships, my self-esteem, morals, and most of all my self-dignity. I knew better, but I didn't do better. I had a decent relationship with my sisters and when this was happening and I wouldn't listen to what my parents or they were trying to tell me, I pushed them away. I stayed away as much as I could because when I was living in sin I was trying to hide and cover myself, ashamed of the sin. I felt like this put a damper on my and my sisters' relationship because I didn't stop doing what they ultimately were asking me not to do.

If I shared anything private with them in confidence and asked them not to say anything to my parents whether it was this situation or any situation growing up, I felt like they didn't respect me enough not to do so. I could never tell them anything without feeling like my parents knew all my secrets even if it wasn't life-threatening. So, I began to shut down and stay to myself and confide only in those that I knew I could trust the older I got into adulthood. Not ideally how I wish things were, but I know it's been better for me this way. But I wish my sisters and I had a better relationship, one as best friends.

After that relationship, I didn't care. I began talking to multiple guys, the majority of which I knew. I was trying to find love in ALL the wrong places. It was a time when I was trying to find it in alcohol, men, clubs, sex, and money. When ultimately that should have been a time for soul searching, loving myself, and devoting my entire being to Jesus, but I was lost and had no real godly mentor that could relate to guide me along the way. Although I never experienced a hangover because I hated the taste of any alcoholic beverage, I was also afraid because my biological father was an alcoholic.

I still tried it multiple times just to feel that buzz, to feel alive at that moment. But in reality, I was dying on the inside. During that time, I was having sexual relations with multiple men in hopes that one of the many would like what I was offering them so much that they would want to keep me. Not realizing that what I was doing was creating a soul-tie with every one of those men I decided to give my body to them for all the wrong reasons. *Soul Tie is a "knitting together" of two souls that refers to a spiritual connection between them. You feel as if you formed a special connection with the other person which usually happens after sexual intercourse. The idea that intercourse creates such ties dates back to antiquity (ANCIENT TIMES).*

That's what I did to myself when I was laying with these different men. Creating soul ties amongst us. But, I thank God for His *restoration* power. I'm grateful He has allowed me to know in His word that I am enough and that he loves me enough. The more you know about God and His love for you, the more you will love the person He has created you to be.

CHAPTER FIVE

HAWAII WAS SUPPOSED TO BE PARADISE

On September 8, 2012, I was working at IHOP as a waitress. A job I had been at for over a decade. I practically raised my daughter at that job. But that particular day I was serving a table of about five individuals. One of the gentlemen that I was serving from the moment he walked in was flirting with me. And of course, I ended up being next in line to get sat with customers. I didn't pay any mind at first. He was with his uncle, his dad, his brother, and a friend. He mentioned I had an accent and I chuckled because in my mind he was the one with an accent. I asked where he was from and he mentioned Texas, which explained the accent. I asked if he was visiting or if he was living here and he said he was visiting his family and that he was in the Navy and on his way to Florida for B school. He continued to flirt, and I didn't pay too much mind. I served them, and he asked if he could have my phone number, I did not give him my phone number and they all walked out except his dad. I thought about it and was wondering what if he's "the one" and I just declined to give him my phone number. His dad came up to me, thanked me for serving them, and before he walked away I said, "you know what, can you give him my phone number?" He agreed and I went on about finishing my day. We texted and talked on the phone almost every day after that and even met up a couple of times before he left for Florida.

Three months later, in December of 2012, after talking and having a long-distance relationship and in-person visits when he was in town, he mentioned he bought me a necklace and asked me to pick it up at a jewelry store at the mall. I went with my daughter, he stayed on the phone with me, and when the sales woman saleswoman gave it to me it was an engagement ring. I was shocked but excited at the same time. He asked me to marry him while we were on the phone and I said, "yes." My family wasn't too fond of him proposing so soon, but they also were supportive of the decisions I made when it came to marrying him. He mentioned to me that he had been married and divorced from someone before me who was only his friend, but they decided to get married in court so that he could obtain more benefits from the military. It didn't bother me, but I was glad he was honest with me about it.

We began planning for a small intimate wedding for the time being. During his time in Florida, he would visit when he could for a few days. He came to visit and he stayed a few nights at my apartment with me. He was in the bathroom showering because we were about to go out. Allowing the insecurity that I struggled with because of past relationships to get the best of me, I decided to search his cell phone. Looking and digging for something to pop up. The mindset I had was, that if I didn't find anything then okay cool, I know there wouldn't have to be a "next time" to search. These thoughts stemmed from continuously being hurt in the past.

I wasn't able to fully get over that hurt and not dealing with it before I went into another relationship was pouring into this relationship. My heart was racing, my hands were shaking, and my knees trembled to the thoughts of what I could see when I open these text messages. Although I did have high hopes that it would be nothing and I would feel foolish. As I scroll through these messages I see one in particular that stood out to me the most. The rage I felt inside that I felt at that moment was as if the beast wanted to unleash within me. I tried to keep my composure and calm down because I didn't want to argue. But, how else would someone feel if they see "sext" messages between your new fiance and another female? It was inappropriate. I wasn't exaggerating. I know I wasn't. I am reading before my very eyes things that the man that claims he was ready to settle down had written to another woman telling her what he wished he could do to her sexually.

When he came out of the shower I know he could see the hurt all over my face. I'm not very good at hiding what I feel. My face told a story of what I was feeling. He asked me what was wrong and I asked him why was he texting someone these types of messages. He mentioned that the female was his friend and that they were goofing around and that it was never his intention to do anything with her. Something in me wanted to believe him and maybe he was telling the truth but I'll never really know. All I know is that I was angry and hurt and nothing at that moment could change that. After we shared our thoughts back and forth about how that was inappropriate and his apologies, I decided to forgive him and pray that he was telling the truth. When in all actuality it was red flag #1 and I ignored it. Red flag #2 was the very first time I had a phone conversation with his mother, she said she wanted to introduce herself to me and get to know me, instead she interrogated me on why I wanted to be with her son. Then she continued to ask me if the only reason I wanted to be with her son was that he was in the military and I wanted him to take care of my kids and me. She was very rude and unkind, throughout our relationship I spoke with her one time, maybe two at the most. I knew he had personal issues with his mom that he never dealt with her and told me not to pay her any mind.

A few weeks go by and we were wedding planning. I asked the pastor from the local church I was attending at the time if he would marry us, but he required us to attend premarital classes with him and his wife before he would agree. He had those requirements because he wanted to ensure we both knew exactly what marriage was from a biblical perspective and God's view of it. That didn't happen because my fiance was not staying local which made it difficult. So, I asked a minister that I have known since I was a little girl, who is like an uncle to me if he would marry us, and he agreed.

On December 28, 2012, we were married in a suite at a hotel room in Cherry Hill, NJ where there were about ten people in attendance including him and me. It was a very small and intimate wedding, but we knew that we wanted a formal wedding. A wedding I have always imagined having where we could celebrate with family and friends, so we planned to have it a few months after we made our marriage official. Since he was in the military he would only be home for a few weeks before he moved to where he was stationed, which was Hawaii. Yes, we were moving to a place that was pretty much paradise and I was ecstatic. He left a couple of days after we got married to prepare for our move. He then came back in March a few months later as we prepared for our formal wedding. At this time I moved in with my sister because I had to ship all of our belongings and my car to Hawaii months in advance so it can be there when we arrived.

My cousin and best friend at the time had planned a bachelorette party for me, but they knew I wasn't interested in any of the craziness that usually happens at bachelorette parties, so they planned dinner and a hotel party with all females, with toys for self-pleasure which I wasn't really into either but I went with it. I got dressed and was getting ready to leave with my sister to head to dinner. As I came down the steps, my fiance looked at me and asked why I had the dress that I had on. I asked him why what was wrong with what I had on? He told me to go upstairs so we could talk. We did. As soon as we walked into the room he gripped both of my arms and slammed me against the door. As I trembled with fear and disbelief, I cried and he instantly snapped out of it and cried, hugged me, and began apologizing. I reminded him that I shared with him when we first started talking that I was assaulted in my last relationship and that I wasn't going to tolerate that again. I was not on this earth to be abused in any way at all. He understood and apologized and said he would never do it again. I believed him. Well, sorta.

About an hour had flown by and I kept getting missed calls from my cousin and my sister kept yelling up the stairs asking if I was ready. I called my cousin back and had to act like everything was okay. I was dressed and ready, but not fully ready because my makeup had smeared, and removing the tears from my eyes was seemingly impossible. I got myself together, went downstairs, and had to act like I was okay that entire night. It was so hard because I wanted to crumble with what had just happened, but I knew that if I shared it with my friends what happened they would not want me to be with someone like that. So, I remained silent and acted like all was well. I tried to enjoy my night as much as possible, but couldn't wait until it was all over.

I forgave him and moved past it. I hoped that the moment he slammed up against the door that it would be the first and the last, but I also knew I was only telling myself that because I wanted it to be. I wanted things to work out between us. Many times in life we want all these things for ourselves and our lives. So much so that we end up trying to force it. We accept others even though we know they're unhealthy or toxic to our lives. We accept them because we may be afraid of being alone. We accept them because we think they're the best thing that ever happened to us, not knowing that God truly has better for us. So, we lower our standards. I felt like my time was ticking and I wanted so badly to be married, have a family, and live the life I always had dreams of living. So, I settled. I hoped and prayed that he would never put his hands on me again as he promised he never would. But with time, and moving me across the world, it only grew worse.

Quick Lesson: Never lower your standards for monetary gain in exchange for eternal matrimony to your purpose or calling in life.

On June 1, 2013, the kids and I relocated to Honolulu, Hawaii. What a dream come true! My husband had been there for a few months before we did to prepare for our arrival. Leaving New Jersey, the only place I ever knew as home was scary, not hard, but scary. Leaving our family and friends was hard, but I knew I needed change. I knew that I wanted to do this and I was ecstatic about doing it. I thought I would get homesick, but I didn't, at all. My husband greeted us at the airport, which to us seemed foreign. It was simple, sort of ran down, quiet, and small. No, we weren't greeted with hula dancers in coconut bras, leis, or colorful shirts. Which is what I kind of expected. Seeing my husband felt like a breath of fresh air. I felt so much peace being there with him and my kids and driving on the way home as he took us for a mini-tour of where we would be residing. We were excited. Hawaii is gorgeous, but it also has projects.

When we arrived at our home, he gave us a tour of the house. A beautiful, brand new remodeled home. We didn't live on the actual military base, but it was military housing in a small community ten minutes from the beach. I loved our home. We were blessed with a three-bedroom, 2.5 baths, living room, family room, large kitchen, dining room, 2 car garage, and fenced-in backyard with a white picket fence. Dream home in paradise, ten minutes from the beach, what else could we ask for? We took the next few days to settle in and do a little bit of sightseeing with some of my husband's military friends and their wives. There were two in particular that with time I became very close with and we all lived near each another. They showed me around a bit more on days our husbands had to work because I was the last one to arrive so they were more familiar with the area than I was. We worked out together, we took turns hosting get-togethers and holidays at one another's houses, and we had many playdates with our kids.

My husband and I had planned pretty early on that we would try and conceive a child, which would be his first biological child. So, that we did. It didn't take long after I arrived in Hawaii, because about a month and a half in I learned that I missed my cycle and found out that I was pregnant. If you do the calculations, I became pregnant in June, which is when we arrived. We wasted NO TIME! Since it was his first child I wanted to do something special for him, so I wrapped a couple of positive pregnancy tests in a diaper and wrapped it in tissue paper for him to open. We recorded this moment and when he opened it up and saw what it was, his eyes lit up and he was extremely joyful. An unforgettable memory, that's for sure. We sold my car that I had shipped from New Jersey and purchased a brand new Ford Explorer so we could all fit because he only owned a motorcycle. With a new bundle of joy coming we needed something comfortable that we all could fit in. We were all excited!

Shortly after that, our amazing, beautiful love story slowly but surely began to turn into a horrible nightmare. His uncle's wife also lived in Hawaii. She was also a military wife, but her husband was on deployment at the time. She and my husband seemed to be rather close but in a weird way. The way they would play around with one another and greeted one another made me feel very uncomfortable and to me, it was on another level of disrespect. When they would greet one another it was a long, extended hug, he would reach back and pinch her butt, and she would giggle and do the same right back to him.

They would start to play fighting and tickling one another so much that they would both end up on the ground and her legs would be wrapped around his waist, they would be giggling, smacking one another's butts, biting, screaming, and so much more, I'm sure you get the picture. This wasn't a one-time thing with them. It was constant, it was annoying and it made me want to explode. I got tired of seeing it and asked him why they "played" that way and explained to him how it made me feel. He became defensive quickly and blamed me for my insecurities and claimed that I was jealous. Me? Jealous of my husband and his auntie? Hmmm.... I think not, it's called having respect for your wife. I questioned myself many times if they ever went further than just this "playing around" thing. Their actions and relationship towards one another were just very peculiar. It seemed like everywhere we were, she was there.

As soon as we moved in he gave her the key to our house without asking me if that was okay for her to have a key to our home. He claimed he gave it to her for emergency purposes, I stated, "Well I would be home the majority of the time, so what emergency purposes would there be?" There was even a time when she came over to visit us and my husband was upstairs in bed, she took it upon herself to climb in our bed with him, she put her backside towards him and was rubbing her butt on him laughing trying to push him off the bed with her butt, and they were both laughing, she asked me to get in the bed with them so we could all relax together and watch a movie, I declined. I sat on my bedroom floor with a look of anger all over my face because if I said something our room would have become a boxing ring, yet again. So, I decided to bite my tongue and wait for her to just leave our home that night and finished with my nightly routine. I'm sure my face and body language said it all and she got the hint, so she wasn't there too long. He made her feel comfortable enough to do that and it wasn't okay.

As the months went on, I looked forward to all the promises he made me when I was still in New Jersey and we were long-distance. He promised we would travel the island together, allowing the kids to experience all the scenery and activities that we could do together, he promised we would go to church together which never happened, I always went along with the kids to this amazing church we discovered very similar to the one we attended back at home. He promised we would pray and read the bible together which we did when we were not living together also, but when we moved together that never happened. He couldn't wait to be a family and do all the things a family would do. But I could count on one hand how many times that happened in the short time we lived there before we were separated.

I tried not to bring up anything that bothered me because I knew it would tick him off and would make him snap. I knew he had issues deep inside from the childhood years that he held on to, but he never took care of those issues. He never wanted to open up about those issues to me, which put a damper on our marriage because in a marriage I knew we were supposed to be open, vulnerable, transparent, and naked and that wasn't limited to clothing.

Yet, he wasn't and I suffered in silence. I bottled everything which was mentally dangerous for me because I wanted to explode with questions I had or concerns that arose within me. I should be able to feel safe with my husband, open, and not feel like I have to walk on eggshells. That wasn't our story. Allowing me into the most vulnerable experiences of your life would allow me to understand him better but I never experienced that with him. That closeness that a union should possess, that bond that a union should have because they shared heart-to-heart moments that you don't share with just anybody.

The intimate moments, even with clothes on. But with him, the intimate moments without clothes on also became an issue. It seemed like every time I wanted to be intimate with him I had to ask him or schedule an appointment with him. It was annoying and I wasn't feeling that at all! When I wanted to be intimate, I WANTED TO BE INTIMATE! Which was a lot, but what husband wouldn't want that? Him, that's for sure. He would lay in bed after saying goodnight to me and turn with his back towards me, he would wrap himself tightly in the blanket implying that he didn't want to be touched or grabbed. It was frustrating!

One morning, I wanted to be intimate with him, but he denied me and told me he wasn't in the mood. So, I got myself together and took the kids to school. Upon arrival, as I walked in I see him sitting on the floor with his laptop on his lap, but he didn't hear me walk in. What I saw next was disheartening. He was watching porn while performing sexual activities on himself. I WAS CRUSHED. What was wrong with me? Why didn't my husband want me? Why did he deny and reject me? Why would he rather watch porn over having me? So many thoughts breezed through my mind. The anger filled up inside me, but I could barely react. He was startled to see me standing there looking down on him in disgust. He quickly cleaned himself up and I sat on the floor crying asking him how he could do that. God created marriage to be pleasurable for the husband and the wife together, not so one could abuse their bodies sexually, which is what this situation was. It was lustful and opened a doorway to bring division between the two of us. That was a hard one to swallow. I sat there crying and shared my heart with him about how I was feeling. His words meant nothing to me at that moment, because I was hurt and disgusted and nothing could change that.

Being in the military meant he had to get up extremely early about four-thirty in the morning to train. I would get up with him, and get his clothes ready for when he would get done training he could come home, shower, and get dressed. I could envision it now. Ironing his clothes, laying it all out, so all he had to do was get dressed and head to work. That was my routine. My heart was to serve him because I knew he worked hard to provide for us. When we first got together we both agreed that we wouldn't put ourselves in a situation where we would be alone with someone of the opposite sex other than our spouses. That is mostly to protect all parties involved. The enemy works in ways that his agenda is to divide a union and he would use the opposite sex to do so. It could begin with no intentions at all, and could lead to becoming friends, to closer friends, to friends that begin sharing personal information, to becoming an ear that understands, to becoming someone you "fall in love with by mistake." That's how tricky the enemies' tactics are.

This is why we must always be aware and vigilant and also not put ourselves in that situation, to begin with. One day he was at work and called me during his lunch. I asked who he was with because I heard voices in the back. He said it was just him and a male co-worker going out for lunch and a female co-worker came along with them. I didn't believe it for one second but tried to. When I know, I know.

But, I left it alone. A few weeks later I found out that it was just him and the female co-worker having lunch together, but he claimed it wasn't anything like that. My thoughts were, "then why did you have to lie about it?" He claims it was because he didn't want me to get upset and think anything about it. I'm sure we could all agree that lying is not the best approach to take in a scenario such as that one. To not get hit I had to stay shut to certain things and began trying to pick and choose my battles wisely.

His anger only grew worse and I began noticing that for him to shut me up or get me to not share my feelings or concerns with him he would always say, "Go ahead and start, I'm not dealing with this, if you talk I will not respond to you." His narcissistic ways tried to muzzle my voice and expected me to just accept every single thing that I couldn't agree with. Yet, his responses would be hateful words, physical actions toward me, and the threat of divorce. Over time I found a few hurtful things. Something led me to look in his email. When I did, I found an email from him to a woman that was very flirtatious and very inappropriate for a married man.

Another time, I found Facebook messages between him and another female that made me question, "Why wasn't I enough for him?" What was I doing so wrong? Since I spoke up about things that bothered me he grew angrier and more hateful toward me. It was as if I didn't know who he was, and that was probably true. We were married so quickly that I didn't even get a chance to really really get to know him. Not every single day was horrible, but the majority of my time in Hawaii and during my pregnancy it was.

He began physically, verbally, and emotionally abusing me, or maybe I just began to notice a more frequent pattern. The worst of those in my opinion was the verbal abuse. As we went to bed he would tell me he hated to hear me breathe, he would tell me he hated me and he doesn't know why he married me, he hated that I provided for him an "already made" family, which meant that he didn't fully accept my kids as his own as he claimed. One day he got so angry with me that he threw a pile of laundry I just folded directly at my face with all of his strength, so hard that it knocked the glasses off my face. Another time, he threw me in the bathtub at six months pregnant, I shoved him with both my hands on his chest, he was so strong he barely moved.

That was the only time I ever came close to defending myself by putting my hands back on him because I was just tired of literally being abused and shoved around. As I walked out of the room to get away from him before he hurt me or my unborn child, even more, he shoved me from the back and I almost ran into the footboard of our bed. My daughter heard me screaming and witnessed him shove me, then he grabbed me and threw me on the bed, and jumped on top of me with his hands around my neck.

He let me go when he heard her screaming, "mommy." He jumped off the bed, and instantly I got up and acted like we were just playing so I had to muster up any strength I had in me to be able to not burst into tears, and say, "Baby, we were only playing, see mommy is okay, I'm okay," with a smile forced on my face, but deep inside I wanted to scream like never before. I was broken. He went into my daughter's room with her and began to tell her that everything was okay and that we were only fooling around. She didn't buy it, not for a second. After he came out of her room, I then went in there with her and my son and locked the door, and was holding them.

That didn't help. He knocked at the door for some time but eventually knew how to unlock it from the outside. And there he was hugging us all and pleading for forgiveness and promising to never do it again. That was a lie. There was another time when he and I were having a debate. I had a bowl of pizza rolls fresh out of the oven and both kids were there eating. He got so mad at me and grabbed a pizza roll, throwing it right into my face. I got upset and ran up the stairs furious, but I didn't want to react and start fighting in front of my kids.

The kids were afraid but just sat there. On several occasions when he would get angry at me he would grab me by both of my wrists, swing me in a circle a few times, then let me go and I would go flying across the room onto the floor. I endured many rug burns on my knees and black and blue wrists on my fair-colored skin, but nothing compared to the words he had written on my heart. When we were younger people would say, "sticks and stones will break my bones, but words will never hurt me." That's one of the biggest lies I have ever heard. Words have been the most damaging thing to me personally. Bruises go away, wounds eventually heal, but the words people spit out at you do more damage. But I know there's nothing my God cannot heal.

I went shopping with a couple of the wives I had gotten close with there. We were looking for workout clothes and they saw my wrists bruised up on both arms. They asked me what happened and I said that we were play fighting and since I'm so light-skinned I bruise up easily. They didn't ask any further questions but I'm sure they weren't believing that story. Later on, I had to eventually open up to them about it because I knew it was only getting worse and I needed help. My family knew nothing because I knew they would be worried and would beg me to come home.

No one knew anything besides my kids and my two friends there. I was ashamed. I didn't know how to share with anyone that I was being abused by my husband, while pregnant, who dragged me halfway across the world and had no intentions of keeping any promises, instead, I became his punching bag and he became my worst nightmare. There were many times the anger I faced would make me sit and ponder how I could get him back, how could I get revenge on all he was doing to belittle, hurt, and abuse me. I had to intercede for myself many times because of the thoughts in my mind of the things that I wanted to do to him that would land me in a prison cell, never seeing my children again. Time after time again the Lord would remind me that he isn't worth it, my children need me, and Romans 12:19 says, *"Do not take revenge, leave room for the wrath of God, vengeance is mine says the Lord."* So as fast as that thought came in several times, that's how quickly the Lord reminded me that I didn't need to get my hands dirty.

I remember a time when he and I were going at it. After we argued he told me to get ready so we can walk over to the pool and let the kids have some fun there and we could both cool off from our heated argument. As I got myself ready in the bathroom, suddenly I heard the house get quiet. I called for them and no one answered. I yelled louder, and still no response. I came out of the bathroom and searched our home and none of them were to be found. I called his phone and he told me they left me.

He was spiteful and told me to get ready so that he can take the kids without me knowing, and left me behind. I never understood how he could be so mean, hateful and evil. I never knew anyone so cold. But his ways towards me allowed me to question more and more why he wanted to marry me. Was it for military benefit purposes like his ex-wife? Was it to feel superior by making someone else inferior? I wondered what was his motive and why it didn't phase him to see me hurt when he acted this way towards me.

As time went on he nagged that we needed help financially and that he was the only one working. So, being the go-getter that I have always known myself to be, I went and applied for a medical assistant position. I was far along in my pregnancy but wore clothes to hide my belly. I was given the position to travel back and forth with a doctor to the main island once a week all expenses paid. It was a great opportunity for us. I asked him for forty dollars to pay for the CPR certification that I had to renew. He argued with me about it and complained that he needed lunch money. I mentioned we had just done food shopping and offered to pack him lunch so we could be able to get to the place of having two incomes. He said, "I am not eating packed lunch from home for the week." And in my mind, I thought, "Oh I guess you're too good for that, yet, you fight that we need more money in the home." I told him never mind and that I would find another way to get the forty dollars for the CPR certification.

He threw the money at me and I threw it back and told him to forget it. I was raised and taught if someone isn't going to give you something with pure and selfless intentions then forget it, I don't want it. That night since I threw the money back at him and told him to forget it, he jumped across the bed, straddled me, put his hands around my neck, and choked me. I could barely breathe and the thought of me never seeing my kids again made me fight even harder to get up. He let me go and I ran downstairs behind the couch again. This time I took pictures of the bruises on my face and neck for proof. He did what he always did and I forgave him once again.

But my patience was wearing thin and I knew I didn't deserve this. I wrote him plenty of emails which I used as proof asking him why he continues to abuse me and begging him to stop. In the emails, he apologizes and says he is going to stop, but it was all broken promises. I didn't know it then, but those emails and plenty of family photos taken on random days showing bruises help my case in the long run.

There's one thing to abuse me, but to feel comfortable enough to abuse my kids became a different story for me. On two different occasions, my daughter who was about nine at the time had gotten a call home from school about her behavior in school and her grades. It was typical kids' stuff, nothing too crazy or alarming. But he allowed his anger to get the best of him. One night as we prepared dinner, the kids sat at the dinner table and I shared with him what happened with her at school. He started yelling at her and since she didn't give him eye contact he slapped her directly across her face, leaving handprints on her face.

Her mouth was left wide open and she fell halfway out of her chair in shock. I was honestly just about as shocked as she was and the anger that ran throughout my bones would have allowed me to have the cops called on me that night. I knew I wasn't ready to be locked up and have my kids stay with an abuser so had to quickly calm myself down. Another time, we began talking about what happened at school and he felt like she was giving him attitude, I was cooking and looking at the stove and he punched her in the stomach and slapped her across the face again, leaving his handprint once again.

I had no problem with him disciplining my children, but when he began putting his hands on their faces and punching them, that drew the line for me, because that was not necessary. I asked him to come upstairs because I wasn't going to fight in front of my kids. We went upstairs and we had a yelling match, I told him he better never lay a hand on my kids again and that he crossed the line with that one. He apologized both times to her, but there should not have had to be a second time. He got angry with my son once who was four at the time and my son ran inside screaming. When I looked down at my son his nose was bleeding and he was crying saying he hit me in my face. I asked him why would he make my son's nose bleed and he claims he didn't mean to. My point was if he wasn't putting his hands on my kids this wouldn't happen. I am their mother and I wouldn't dare slap their faces the way he thought was okay to do in disciplining a child.

The pain I felt like a mother to have to know that my babies were hurting because someone who was supposed to love them, hurt them. Thankfully, those were the only three instances that he hit my kids. I think he got the point. For me it was different, he wouldn't get the point.

I loved being the wife to please him, but he rejected me time and time again, and I still tried. I was seven months pregnant and I put on lingerie so when he arrived from work I was ready to be intimate with him. I walked up to him, hugged and kissed him. He stopped, looked down, pulled back, and said, "Maybe you should wear that after the baby is born." I felt beautiful carrying another life inside of me, but he thought otherwise. I picked up my courage and face that hit the floor walked away and went into our bedroom walk-in closet to cry it out. That closet has held many many of my unnumbered tears.

That was my place. My place where I would just go to cry and let it all out. My closet was my safe space, but when I couldn't get to my closet because he was in the room, I would hide behind the couch in a corner or in the downstairs bathroom. It became almost like a routine. He would get angry with me. threaten to divorce me, put his hands on me, I would run out the room, run downstairs behind the couch, he would turn the hallway light on, quietly creep down the stairs as I watched to see how far he was from me, he would find me, tell me to come out so we could talk. I would come out and he would say the same thing, that he was sorry, he won't do it again, I would forgive him, and then it would happen all over again.

It became mentally, physically, and emotionally draining, but I loved him and prayed he would seek help and change for us all, most importantly himself. He agreed to go to marriage counseling and said he wanted to work things out, so I made an appointment with the counselors. We both arrived at our appointment together and walked into the room with the counselor. Before we began he asked if he could get a separate counselor. I questioned why would we do counseling separately if it was marriage counseling. He said because he didn't want to do counseling. I asked then why would you agree to do counseling and now you're saying something different.

His response was, that he only agreed so that I could shut up and stop crying like a baby about it. I wasn't sure how much more I could take of this back and forth but I knew my vow was made to God and him that no matter what I will fight for our marriage and so I did. We left that session and I spoke with one of the counselors for a one-on-one session. It didn't help if I'm being honest, I felt like at this point nothing would help, if he wasn't going to be willing. I knew at this point I had to call my dad and give him a heads up about what was going on. It was going on way too long and I had held this from my family far too long. I knew for my family the time was ahead of ours, so I broke night waiting for it to be about 5 am for my dad because I knew he would be up. I called him and told him what was going on, except I didn't tell him I was being abused physically.

I knew if I told my family I was being physically abused they would have found a way to end up in Hawaii to get me and I wasn't ready for that. All I told him was that things weren't working out between us and I needed him to speak to my husband. He did, but my husband wasn't trying to receive anything wise my dad had to say. My dad told me the moment I know it was time to come home, then they would be waiting for me. I'm blessed my family was able to see me again because many women don't make it out of situations similar to this one, alive.

One evening his auntie came over to our house with her kids and our kids were all playing together in the playroom. He and his auntie began having a conversation about the past and how he visited her once years before and how they went out to the club. Then he took it a bit further and started talking about how the girl he messed with that night at the club, his aunt's friend had a fat butt. I was standing there and they seemed to have forgotten because the conversation grew even more inappropriate and I was disrespected, you could probably see flames coming out of my head because of how mad I was.

His aunt told him to chill because I was standing there and it was inappropriate. He disagreed and I spoke up and said, "actually it is, if you want to have that conversation have it when I'm not around." He got defensive, I told him to let's go upstairs and talk away from our guests, but instead, he wanted to make a scene in front of our guests. He grabbed me by my arm and pulled me upstairs. While he was dragging me up the steps I told him I didn't want to go and that I would rather stay downstairs until he calmed down. He continued to drag me in front of the kids and his aunt. His aunt knew it was about to escalate, so she followed us, yelling at him to take his hands off of me.

He didn't. We get into our room, he shuts and locks the door and he starts yelling and screaming at me about how insecure and jealous I am. I was so embarrassed but mostly angry. I sat by my bed on the floor and wept because I couldn't believe he was doing this with all the kids downstairs and his auntie right in our room. He was screaming all types of names at me and cursing at me. Everything you can think of in the book, he called me. I sat there and cried. He walked up behind me and slapped me right across the back of my head and kept on egging me on to get up and "talk" since I so badly wanted to talk.

Except he wanted to yell, scream, fight and hit me. I didn't do anything but sit there and cry, his auntie came and sat behind me on the floor. She rubbed my back and my head and told him he needed to stop putting his hands on his pregnant wife, she told him to get out and calm down. His last words to me that night in front of his aunt were, " You watch, you're gonna die in this house, keep on." I didn't take those words lightly from someone who was in the military, training to be a navy seal, along with having a custom-made rifle locked away in our bedroom closet. I was trembling with terror. The only thing that ran through my mind was that I needed to get me and my kids out alive, but how? That night we went to bed after things calmed down. I barely slept a wink. He went to work and I emailed him and asked when he arrived home could we talk. He never answered me.

That evening, it was exactly one week away from our first wedding anniversary and a few days before Christmas. I waited for him to return home and as time grew closer to his normal time to be home I grew more anxious. Time passed and he was never this late arriving home from work. I called and his phone went straight to voicemail. Over and over and over. The more I called, the more nervous and anxious I felt. Something was not right and I felt desperation hover over me. I left texts, voicemails, and emails. NOTHING! I called his aunt and no answer. It was close to 10 pm and I wanted to scream because I had no response at all, from any of them. I called one of my friends who lived close to me and asked her if she could watch the kids so I can go to the hospital because the longer I didn't hear from him, the more I cried, and the sharper the pains became in my stomach. I was afraid I would have a miscarriage from the abuse and the severe stress I was under. She watched my kids and to the military hospital, I went.

They began checking me and had to run the tests a second time because they thought I was leaking amniotic fluid because they thought my body was trying to go into labor too soon. I was there for hours waiting for the results. I was alone and scared. Time passed and the nurse asked me if I was being abused at home because she saw a bruise on my arms, from the night he dragged me up the stairs. I dropped my head and began to cry. She said you don't have to try and protect your husband, tell us if you need help. I cried even more.

I shook my head, yes, and I'm sure she saw the fear in my face. I wanted to protect him, I'm not going to lie. I didn't want him in trouble which is why I never went to the police about it before that. I just dealt with it because I didn't want to lose him and I hoped that he would get the help he knows he needed and promised he would get. Instantly they called the military domestic violence representatives.

I was terrified because she began to tell me that once they are called, they have to tell his commanding officer and it will escalate. I asked her not to take it that far, but it was too late. They spoke with me and got all the information they needed from me. I knew he would be furious and that this wouldn't go well for us. That year I spent that Christmas alone with my kids on the beach, just us three. The gifts we bought them together they opened. It was beautiful to spend with them on the beach and a nice surprise for them, but my heart felt empty. It was lonely.

Once his commanding officers were involved, it was downhill from there. Since that night he never slept in that home with us again. He abandoned us. He would come sporadically at all hours of the night, but he would park his motorcycle down the street so we wouldn't hear him coming into the house. At this point, I began sleeping with the kids in our bed altogether with a nightstand blocking the door because I wasn't sure what his intentions were. If he had plans to harm us, try and take my kids from me, or worse try to kill us. So I protected us and blocked the door so we could wake up when we heard him coming in the room by pushing the nightstand over.

I spent many hours in police stations in town and on the military base putting in for restraining orders and police reports. His commanding officers reached out to me to plan the days they could come with him to move his belongings that he needed daily out because he eventually was restricted from entering the home alone and needed to be escorted. He knew that us wearing our wedding bands was huge for me as I shared with him when we first got married. The first day he came to get his stuff he walked down the stairs as I watched from the couch. He ran his hand down the stair railing and I saw that he took his wedding band off. I knew at that moment he was done.

But, I still prayed he would have a change of heart and we could work things out. He lost the privilege to bear arms for threatening to kill me and was under review for abusing me. He was found guilty of the abuse with all the proof I provided to them and he was livid. We attended another counseling session together and after lots of praying I was hoping he would seek help, we would continue to attend counseling sessions together and work on our marriage. Well, that didn't happen. We walked into the counseling session. He sat beside me, the counselor asked who wanted to go first. He asked if he could.

He looked me in my face and said, "I hate you, I never want to see you again, you and I are done, there will never be another us again, I want a divorce, go back home to your family, you tried to take everything I worked so hard for and if I have to choose I am choosing my career over this family." And he did. He meant what he said. As if I wasn't shattered into a trillion pieces already. He then walked out of the room, I sat there with my head held low crying as the counselor sat there trying to comfort me. He never gave me a chance to speak, a chance to say what I had to say, a chance for closure, a chance to try. I didn't get an option, I didn't have a choice. It wasn't mutual. He chose for me.

My heart was aching and all I wanted at that moment was to feel his touch, his hug, his embrace, his love one last time. Instead, I felt his wrath, his anger, his fury and I fell apart. I have never prayed so hard in my life before. I was always a strong, independent woman, except I didn't feel anything near strong and barely felt woman enough. I was robbed of everything or so it felt like I did, everything including my self-worth. I spent hours upon hours crying out to the Lord, asking him why, pleading with him, begging him to fix my broken marriage, to allow my husband to see that we could mend things no matter how bad they looked.

After we split up, I began seeing pictures that he was tagged in with two females from his job, one that he went to lunch with and another woman. They were hugged up with him and they had seemed to be partying. They tagged him so I would be able to see it. To hurt me as if I wasn't hurt enough.

I cried out to God to fix me and make me strong for my kids because there were times I didn't even feel enough for them. I stood on the bible verse Jeremiah 29:11 during that season of my life and it's still my favorite verse. *For I know the plans I have for you declares the Lord, plans to prosper you and not to harm you, plans to give you hope and a future.* I held so tightly to that word and meditated on it day and night because as much as I questioned God on why he would allow me to go across the world in marriage to then have it crumble right before my eyes, I knew He must have had a plan. I must have been out of His will in the first place. Trying to do things MY way, instead of His way. Then having to learn the hard way.

The next few weeks for me were literal hell. I couldn't eat anything, I couldn't sleep and I could barely take care of my kids. All I wanted to do was curl up in a ball and cry. In that season, I began experiencing night terrors. I would try to sleep but then would wake up abruptly by a nightmare. I would jump up and find myself sweating, with my stomach in knots, ending up in the bathroom, sweating, feeling like I was going to pass out and I was scared because I was alone with two young children. It was hard to sleep.

Having to stare at the 16x20 large canvas wedding photo that sat above our headboard, remembering my why and not being able to figure out his why was torture. I wanted to be held like that again, like in our photo. Loved like he promised he would love me. I couldn't figure out his why, only he could do that. The memories that replayed over and over in my head. Our wedding, moving to Hawaii, our pregnancy announcement, buying the first car that we owned together, decorating our home, the moments that were beautiful for us. I just couldn't get it out of my head. He only made it to about two of our doctor's appointments with me. The excitement he once felt about becoming a father suddenly turned into a disconnect. I went through that pregnancy pretty much as a single woman.

The rest of the appointments I went to alone. I had to visit my doctor more frequently than usual. She was very concerned for me. My time with my doctor partially became a therapy session for me and she poured into me. Allowing me to know I was worth more than being abused, by a man who claimed to love me and who claimed he wanted to seek help but never did. She didn't know it and I barely knew it then but God was using that doctor to pour into me mightily in that season.

She was kind, and as I think back on it she probably carried my burdens along with her home, that's how sincere she was. She did and said everything she could to get me to see that at that moment when all I was worried about was my marriage, she wanted me to see that my unborn fetus was more important. I began losing weight, she was concerned about these night terrors, and many times I couldn't feel my baby move. I invited him to the appointments, but he constantly declined. He didn't want any part of us, none at all and I wished I didn't care, but I would be lying. I wanted to fight for our marriage no matter what and felt like I failed God if I divorced.

He decided it was best for my kids and me to go back home to New Jersey because he felt his career was on the line. My family thought it was best we come home as well because they were tired of worrying about me. I didn't want to go. I loved Hawaii. I loved living there. I felt an enormous amount of peace there aside from my abusive situation. I truly felt at home. I contemplated splitting up and going my separate way, but staying there. But it was way too expensive for me to live there alone, with three kids and not having an income at the time. My family begged me, and so did he.

I told him if he wanted us to leave he had to put in military orders for us to get all of our stuff shipped back because I shouldn't have to come out of pocket for it all. I also told him if I moved back to New Jersey he better never come looking to work things out with me ever again. My doctor had to put in an emergency leave for us to be able to fly back home quickly. I had to leave all of our belongings behind. All we had was the clothes on our back, a small suitcase, a lot of hurt and a lot of pain. For me, I also had a burden of embarrassment and shame to carry along with me.

I didn't feel comfortable leaving all my belongings in the house, but I had no choice. The movers packed and moved all of our stuff and sent it back to New Jersey. He knew what he and I discussed about who would keep what but when my belongings arrived in New Jersey he did not keep his word. I wanted to fight for the stuff that he kept, but then I realized those are all materialistic things and it wasn't worth it. I knew that my and my kids' safety and health were the most important thing. I knew that God would provide all our needs as the faithful God that He is. In time He did. We lacked nothing. We may not have everything we had, but we do have everything we need. For that, I praise my God for being my Jehovah Jireh, The Lord that Provides.

Here is the lesson:

Sometimes we fight for what we want instead of fighting for what we need.

Ask yourself this question, is what I'm fighting for a want or a need? When you figure out what it is

that you need, God will always provide your wants and heart's desires according to His will.

Lean on God for what you need, and according to His perfect will, He will give you what to want.

CHAPTER SIX

_____

LETTER TO HIM

Dear Ex-husband.

I have never gotten closure...I still don't have all the answers as to why you did what you did to me, or what you did to us. I know I will never get the answers to the questions I have and it's something I learned to be okay with. I have forgiven you, not just for you, but for me. I can only hope and pray that you realized whatever caused so much pain for you, whatever has allowed you to be angry, bitter, and hateful to address it so you can find healing and move on to being a better man most importantly for you.

And if you already have, Praise God. I was angry when everything first happened because I couldn't understand why you would marry me, move us to Hawaii, and promise us that you would always be there no matter what, yet when things got shaky. After all, I wanted to put a stop to your abuse you abandon us. I no longer give place to the devil by remaining angry with you.

Wherever you are in the world I want to say, thank you. Because of you, the Lord has placed me right where I belong to be able to find the one whom my soul loves. I can only pray you have forgiven yourself for all you have done to us. We are okay. We are loved. We are well taken care of.

Genesis 50:20 You intended to harm me, but God intended it for good to accomplish what is now being done, saving many lives.

Genesis 45:5 And now, do not be distressed and do not be angry with yourselves for selling me here, because it was .to save lives that GoS sent me ahead of you.

I learned that :

Unforgiveness hinders my relationship with God.

You are God's son.

If I stay angry, it gives place to the devil. It's a tactic from Satan to steal the presence of God.

If I want to do some real heavy evangelism, I must forgive those who hurt me the most.

When I forgive I'm not only setting you free, but I'm also setting myself free, you can't have control over me anymore.

Thank you,

I am exactly where I am supposed to be.

CHAPTER SEVEN

FORGIVENESS BLOG

Could forgiveness be that one thing that's holding you back from a life of peace and joy? For the most part, you may not be okay with forgiving the person who may have hurt you.

You may have been so hurt that it almost seems impossible to even think about forgiving that person who did you wrong, who hurt you, or even betrayed you. You carry bitterness, hatred, unforgiveness, anger, rage and so many other things because you just can't seem to let it go and move past the hurt. I get it, trust me. I, too have been hurt, many times before. I have realized that you can't change anyone, but you can change how you deal with that person.

Whether it's loving them from afar or even forgiving them and giving it to God so you can live a life of peace. Did you know that forgiveness is more for you than it is for them?

Think about it... if you harbor unforgiveness, you are the one holding on to that issue, you are the one constantly going through the rage and anger in your mind when you think of who hurt you. You're the one not at peace and God promised us a life of peace... a peace that passes all understanding.

Philippians 4:7 And the peace of God, which transcends all understanding, will guard your hearts and your minds in Christ Jesus.

We could go weeks or even months without even thinking of that person, but boom the enemy throws a dart, and all of a sudden all those messy feelings that you thought were gone just rose again and you have no clue where they came from.

You weren't even prepared to emotionally handle all these crazy thoughts again. But that is how the enemy works to try and distract you and most of us do fall into it, sometimes unknowingly. Don't allow the enemy to rob you of your peace. Instead, make a shift and go into a place of worship and enter into God's presence.

God's presence is what allows me to clear my mind and give me a sense of peace. He constantly reminds me that He is here and I can feel that He is here, all I have to do is go to Him. It's a place I never want to come out of once entered. Let that be constant for your life.

That place of security. That place of peace. That place of hope. That place of love. That place of comfort. Do you want it?! I remember many times going into church and feeling upset, hurt, frustrated, angry, or not myself. But as soon as worship is over I feel like the tons of bricks I walked into church with have just fallen off. I left it at the altar.

Forgiveness... He does not hold it back from us. No matter how many times we fail, He is constantly forgiving us and throwing all we have done into the Sea of Forgetfulness.

Micah 7:18-19 Who is a God like you, who pardons sin and forgives the transgression of the remnant of his inheritance? You do not stay angry forever but delight to show mercy. You will again have compassion on us; you will tread our sins underfoot and hurl all our iniquities into the depths of the sea.

Isn't he a good and gracious God?!

Josilyne Thomas 8/6/19

CHAPTER EIGHT

WOMAN, BE LOOSED!

As a teenager and young adult, I would use the words, '"I have anxiety." When in reality, I was just nervous. But the words we speak are powerful. ***Proverbs 18:21 Death and life are created with our words. The tongue has the power of life and death, and those who love it will eat its fruit.*** So we must be careful what we allow to come out of our mouths. I never knew what anxiety felt like until I traveled to Hawaii all alone for my divorce for the second time.

The first time I traveled for our court hearing I wasn't alone, but the hearing was postponed, which meant more time wasted for nothing, and more money spent on another flight that was not reimbursed. Traveling alone, long layovers due to hazardous weather conditions, the reason for this trip, seeing "him" all over again, twelve-hour flight, it all had me worked up. I began feeling something I never felt before. ANXIETY!!!!!!

My heart was racing, my eyes felt like they were going to bulge, and I felt scared, nervous, unsettled, and worried. On the outside, I seemed fine and looked okay, but on the inside, I felt like a wreck. I stayed with one of my friends and her family that I met when lived in Hawaii. I'm grateful I had a place to stay during my short visit, which allowed at least a little bit of comfort. I tossed and turned the night before the court date.

A million thoughts ran through my mind about what could happen or what would happen at least that's what it seemed. What if after court he tried to harm me knowing I was alone? What if the judge decided something I didn't agree with and I'm hundreds of miles away from my family and support system? It all had me overwhelmed and felt like too much to bear. The anticipation kept me up, no matter how hard I tried to fall asleep. I wanted this to all be over with so that I could move on with my life and feel some sort of normalcy again, especially within my mind. I was cning home, I prayed that those feelings would shortly dissolve because I wasee again." But they didn't. The anxious thoughts that consumed me became more intense. It was almost as if I had no control over my body or my mind. I had Xanax that my doctor prescribed previously for my flight in case I needed them. I didn't use them but, coming back home I felt as if I needed them to get relief from what felt like a nightmare. I couldn't shake the feeling no matter how hard I tried, what I did, or how hard I prayed.

So, I tried a pill. It helped me relax and allowed me to sense relief. I could laugh again, I spent time with my kids, and I wanted to be around others. But when the medication wore off it left me feeling like I needed another or else, I was crippled. I had a fear of leaving the house, socializing, going out in big groups, and being near my extended family. It was horrible. No one knew what I faced during this season of my life except those that I lived with and saw every day. The more medication I took, the more I felt like I needed it to be able to allow me to feel like I could breathe again, even if it was just for 4-6 hours. It was as if a truck was weighing on my chest. I thank God for my children and Kenny who at the time was my boyfriend.

They were extremely patient and it's exactly what I needed because I wasn't sure how to control what was happening to me. I also wasn't sure how long I would be feeling this way, nor did I know what I could do to help myself. All I knew was that I was needed and I had to do something to get better. At the time, Kenny was teaching dance and we traveledance, andmpetition our kids competed in away from home.

My doctor at that time had begun trying to move me from Xanax to a depression medication because Xanax was more of a short-term medication. I voiced to my doctor that I wasn't depressed, I was just anxious because I was facing a divorce that I wasn't sure how to handle. He expla in ed that anxiety and depression go hand in hand. I disagreed with that because I didn't feel depressed, but I did agree to try out the medication. I was instructed to take a half pill of the anti-depressant for the first day but then the full tablet the next day. I took half when we were at the competition and I never want to feel what I felt at that moment.

In about five minutes I was shaking nervous and crying hysterically. It felt like a dark, heavy cloud of sadness hovered over me at that moment. It was almost as if I reached up, I could touch the cloud that's how close and real it felt. I was embarrassed and ashamed. Kenny couldn't help me at that moment because he was busy getting the kids prepared for the competition. I remember walking outside with one of the dance moms and she comforted me. Smoms, andsted that I take a Xanax just so it can get me through that moment of being at the competition so I could feel competition, so and it relieved me.

But I didn't like medication, to begin with, I never did. It was in that moment where I was just over it all and wanted to feel like myself again. But what would that look like? How do I do that? I felt helpless. I didn't want to live because I couldn't enjoy life due to the anxiety controlling me. I was desperate!

How I broke loose: I began seeing this Cricut machine being advertised and I wanted it to begin doing crafts. We didn't have a lot of money at this time, but I asked my husband anyway if we could buy it. I told him I could start selling things and make the money back. So, we went ahead and bought it after much hesitation. Within a few months, I was learning, creating, selling, and m,aking the money back. This machine was ogettingf the things that saved my life. It kept me busy and interested in learning more and more. To top it off, the items I was creating and selling allowed me to put a smile on other people's faces, which allowed me to see that I did still have a purpose.

Luke 13:12 When Jesus saw her, he a called her forward and said to her, "Woman, you are set free from your infirmity."

CHAPTER NINE

ANXIETY BLOG

ANXIETY HAS NO FACE!

The definition of anxiety is a feeling of worry, nervousness, or unease, typically about an imminent event or something with an uncertain outcome. In other words, when you feel like you have no control, anxiety comes into play. I began to feel anxious when I was going through my divorce at 28 years old. I lived a great portion of my life never really being able to speak on what anxiety was or what it made people feel like. Until I couldn't control the fact that I was being forced to divorce someone that was physically and mentally abusive to me. It took a toll on my mind because when you're being forced to do something you didn't have planned and something you have no control over that decision it affects you.

My anxiety was so bad that I didn't want to leave the house, I felt fear throughout my entire body, I was a nervous mess, and I was so unhappy and lost. The Doctors prescribed me medicine that only made me feel happy and calm for a small amount of time then I yearned for more medicine. I took that pill just to feel some type of normalcy and to be able to mother my kids because without it, I just wanted to lie in bed. I found myself relying on the medication more than my God.

The more medication I took, the more I felt I needed. Sometime after, the Doctor's prescribed me something a little more long-lasting and that didn't work out for me at all. I took half a pill and I was done. The anti-depressant actually made me feel depressed and I wasn't depressed, I was anxious. I remember clearly the day I took half of that pill, all I could do was cry. I felt horrible. I was exhausted mentally. It was a Wednesday, December 3, 2014, after service, that I spoke with my pastor about what I was going through. We shared conversations about my situation and how this medication was affecting me. I remember him saying, "the more you take some of these medications, the more they make you yearn for them.

The more you feel like you need them. They'll help solve one problem, but then will cause another problem. He informed me some people take medications that they need and they do well, some don't. I had to make a decision. Do I stop? Do I keep going? Do I want to rely on this medicine forever? No, I don't.. personally, for me, I just hate taking medicine in general. Give me all the natural stuff as much as possible.

On December 5, 2014, I swallowed the very last Xanax that I had ever taken and decided that it ended there. Was it easy? NO! Was it hard? Absolutely, YES! I felt as if I had no control over my emotions at all. Thank God for the patient man he gave me (my current husband) because he was so patient with me through all of these different challenges I faced. It was a roller coaster and he supported me through it all. You may be asking, have I stopped feeling anxious altogether? The answer is no. I haven't. There are times when anxiety still creeps up on me.

What I do to help cope;

• **Verbally claim full healing over my body by faith**

• **I have done a better job of relying on God to get me through that very moment**

- **Remember what triggered that feeling of anxiety, because most of the time there's a trigger**

- **Speak to myself out loud, pray scriptures, worship, and do something creative that will take my mind off of what I'm feeling in that current moment. Most of the time it's about something I can't control that I try to have control over.**

- **The bible tells us to cast all of our cares on Him because He cares for us. (1 Peter 5:7) The bible also tells us, to be anxious for NOTHING, but in everything by prayer and supplication with thanksgiving let your requests be made known to God. He is our help!!!!!!**

Anxiety doesn't have a face! But it also doesn't have a place! Most of the time you can see someone and never even know they are struggling with anxiety. That's why it's important to be kind to everyone you meet. You have no clue what silent battles they are facing. Many times my anxiety left me isolating myself, not wanting to have conversations, not wanting to go out in large crowds, not wanting to socialize, and feeling like everyone can tell that I had anxiety just by looking at me.

Which in turn, made me more anxious, my heart would beat very quickly, I was fatigued and nervous, and I was even afraid to talk to anyone about feeling anxious thinking they would say, "you're a follower of Christ, how are you anxious?" But it's okay because there were people in the bible who suffered from anxiety... Martha, Job, and King David to name a few. Thanks be to God, He has been working in me because the anxiety in my life isn't that extreme anymore.

There are times I do still struggle with anxiety and moments the enemy will try to put in my mind that the medication I used to take is still needed. But he is a liar!!!!!! I am awaiting my full deliverance and healing from anxiety. But I'm gonna wait on You Jesus! I'm not turning back now! I believe God is helping me get through these moments, teaching me to stop trying to have control over everything, to be more patient in the waiting, and stop trying to get ahead of Him & to solely rely on Him.

I don't know what's that thing that's making you anxious, but I believe our God is Healer over ALL and He has not left your side even in the struggles of your anxiety. When no one seems to understand what you are facing, God most certainly does! Run to the throne room and lay it all at the altar! Your time is coming for full healing!

Speak it over your life and wait on Jesus! Reflect on this:

1. Do you want to be made whole?

2. Do you trust God FULLY or do you trust the control you think you have more?

3. What are some things you can do to take your mind off the anxiety when it comes?

4. Are you willing to speak scriptures over your life rather than keep on repeating the fact that you deal with anxiety?

CHAPTER TEN

ALL IN

I moved back home to New Jersey, in February 2014. My two oldest kids and I came back with the clothes we had on our backs, one small bag each, a lot of hurt, a lot of pain, confusion, and much humility. We also came back with grateful hearts knowing that we were still alive, and well, and with the determination that we were going to find our healing. My parents opened up their home to us until we got back on our feet. I finally opened up to my family about the physical abuse in Hawaii and they were very grateful I was blessed to se another day.

I had no car, no house furniture, and no money. I felt like everything I ever owned and worked so hard for was stolen from me. It was a Job moment for me. In the bible, everything was taken from Job. He lost his children, his possessions, and his health. Yet, he still praised God. I had no right to be angry at God. After all, I know He had given me the signs and red flags to not marry this man and I still went ahead and did it, because it's what I wanted for my life. As an adult woman, I didn't want to have to move back home, but I am thankful that I had a place to go to be able to build up what had been taken and lost from me. During this time my family was very supportive of me. For me, it was a clear picture of humility at its finest.

When we knew we were definitely moving back home I reached out to Aliyana's dance teacher Kenny that she danced with since she was 7 years old and mentioned we were moving back home, and she wanted to start dancing again. I knew that was her outlet. I knew it was what she needed most at that moment in her life. Kenny said he would love to have her join again, and she could just start dancing on the scheduled rehearsal days without re-auditioning again.

He asked me why we were moving back and if everything was okay. I told him the short version, straight to the point of the story, and he mentioned he too had a pretty recent break-up. Kenny knew I was unemployed moving back home and offered me to do some sales work for him along with a few others, and we would get a commission off of it to make a little cash. I agreed, and we had a couple of business meetings together to discuss further what the goal was moving forward. They say God works in mysterious ways right? Well, He sure does and His plan is always the best plan.

It was close to my birthday and my best friend was supposed to take me out to dinner to celebrate my special day. She ended up canceling last minute, and I was a bit sad because I was looking forward to it. Kenny and I had been texting from time to time, and he asked what I was up to. I mentioned my best friend was supposed to take me out but ended up canceling. So he asked if he could take me out for my birthday because he was free. With no hesitation, I said, "yes". I mean, "why not?" So we went out. Our very last impromptu first date! That wasn't even really a date. And that's where our journey to forever began.

He picked me up, and we went out to this amazing Thai restaurant that we still go to every year as a reminder of where it all began. I still remember where we sat as if it were yesterday. I remember when we ordered our drinks my straw wrapper was folded up into the design of a rose. It was very creative and beautiful and made my heart smile. I took it home with me and saved it for memories. To think that the entire time we were there just as friends, not realizing it truly was the beginning of both of our happily ever afters. While we allowed the Thai food to fill our bellies, we enjoyed the night to the fullest and it filled our hearts. Kenny was such a gentleman that evening and even opened the car door for me. Which was just one more thing I admired about him.

After that night, we continued to text often. He began flirting through text and I wasn't opposed to it. What allowed me to know he was really into me was when he sent me a text bragging about his cooking skills and I replied, "I'll be the judge of that." So, we agreed that he would pick me up, and cook me dinner, and we did just that. It was delicious as he knew it would be. We liked each other, A LOT and it showed! But I was skeptical because I knew for sure I wasn't ready to move on after being beaten on in Hawaii and feeling as if I would never want to be with anyone else. At least not this soon. I knew Kenny was a great guy and I knew that I didn't want to be alone forever. But, I also knew my heart needed the necessary time to heal the wounds that someone else put there, but never took accountability for, and so I remained scarred, with no closure, no last words, no goodbye. Nothing. Just abandonment.

I was careful, very careful, but I also didn't want to miss out on someone amazing that God had for me all because of someone else's mistakes. It didn't help that my father wasn't too pleased with me seeing Kenny. He didn't really know Kenny, but from a father's perspective he was in "protective daddy mode." After all, he had seen and heard that I had to deal with in Hawaii. He knew I was hurt and that alone, hurt him. So he wanted me to be cautious. I was upset that my father didn't accept Kenny so early on. But, could I blame him? Usually, my mother is the one against things like this. This time it was my father and my mother was pretty open to it. Later on, I found out that she told my dad, "Let her be, what if this is truly the man that God has for her." Momma's know best!

Kenny and I continued to date and as time progressed, so did our feelings for one another. We would stay on the phone all hours of the night. Sometimes, until 3 a.m. Sometimes, until 5 a.m. if it was really serious. Many arguments were even had until the sun rose because everything wasn't always perfect. We were both broken individuals that God used as two vessels to display His love and grace through. Nonetheless, I did what God had planned for us. We were just taking it day by day, or as Kenny would say, "just let everything happen naturally."

Kenny had his own apartment and most days when I would go over to spend time with him and watch movies, we would fall asleep and I would just stay overnight there. My dad was really bothered by that and gave me a piece of his mind a few times. Again, he wasn't wrong, but I still did it anyway. It got to the point where I pretty much lived there with him because the kids and I were always with him. I washed his laundry, cooked, cleaned, and we had gatherings with our friends and their families.

It was great! One day while Kenny and I were driving my husband called, we weren't legally divorced at the time, but we were legally separated. I put him on speakerphone, so we could both hear what he had to say because I was already invested in Kenny and nothing he had to say was a secret. I heard him out, and he said he wanted to be a family again, he asked if I could move to Hawaii to be with him and work things out. He apologized for everything he did or said and promised he was serious this time. He told me he loved me and that he finally realized that he wanted to work on our marriage.

Kenny and I chuckled and shook our heads. I heard him out and I told him that I couldn't. I reminded him that I told him if I moved back to New Jersey he better not come looking for me or try to work things out then. I told him he missed out, he had his chance, and I moved on and was beyond happy, and he could proceed with the divorce that HE filed claiming that our marriage was "irretrievably broken." Which I did not agree with. So, he did.

A few months after I began staying at Kenny's place more often and my dad called me early on Easter Sunday. He said our family was having Easter dinner, and he invited Kenny to join us. My eyes lit up as I shared with Kenny. We were shocked because he was not happy with the fact that I was dating Kenny so soon after my break-up in Hawaii. We agreed to go, and we had an amazing time. At one point my father and Kenny stepped out to have a heartfelt conversation and inside I was nervous, trying to figure out what was being said between them both.

A few times I took a peek and saw cordial faces, and positive body language, so I knew that it couldn't have been going bad at all. Later that evening Kenny shared that all went well, and they both were able to share their hearts with one another. My dad shared his concerns and Kenny understood and shared that he was not looking to hurt or take advantage of me. Instead, he wanted to truly see where this would go with us and promised my father that he would take great care of me and the kids. My dad gave us his blessings and from that point on, he accepted Kenny into our family and wanted to give him an opportunity to prove himself.

Kenny and I continued to date without feeling like we had a weight on our shoulders. There were still a few people who questioned how could I be dating him and why because of their own personal reasons or opinions, but we didn't allow ourselves to hinder what we knew we had. Which was a special kind of love that neither one of us experienced before. In life, there will be people who will always have something to say, but you have to have the confidence in knowing that if God said it, He will bless it regardless of the naysayers. Some thought it was kind of awkward that I was dating my daughter's dance teacher. I get it. But again, it wasn't planned, and we went with the flow with what felt right, nothing rushed nor out of spite.

God has a way of shocking people, including us. We would have never expected to be together, at all. We loved being around one another and it all felt so right. We had several conversations with my daughter who for her was a little weird about me dating her dance teacher. We were very open and honest with her and were very supportive of her feelings. With time, we knew it wouldn't be so weird, and not long after everything was fine with her. She was just happy that I was happy and treated with respect after all she witnessed in Hawaii.

The beginning of our relationship was great but challenging. I had come into a relationship with trust issues because I didn't allow myself time to heal or get over what happened to me in Hawaii. After all, we began dating fresh out of my arrival back from Hawaii. We had many heated arguments because it was very hard to get over the trauma I had just gone through. I would constantly look through Kenny's phone just looking and waiting to find something that wasn't supposed to be there.

Time and time again I would feel dumb because what I expected to find wasn't there. I thought that what I went through with other men was what I would go through with Kenny. So, I almost hoped to find something to blame him for, so I could say, "I told you so, I knew all you men were the same." I felt like I wasn't worth anything at this point because of the words I accepted that my ex-husband had spoken to me. I would ask Kenny, "Why do you want to be with me? I am nothing, you don't want to be with anyone like me, so just leave." Hoping that he would say, "You know what, you're right," and would walk away.

But no matter how much I tried to push his buttons, get him to see all my flaws rather than the best of me, he still wouldn't leave. That showed me that he was a strong man. Did he deserve that in order to show me that he was there for the long haul, that he was willing to stay, that he was willing to be there no matter what? No, he didn't deserve it.

If you ask me to give someone else advice on this situation I had been in, I would say to heal before moving on.

I was blessed to have gotten a man with so much patience. If it had been someone with very little patience, we probably, most likely would not have worked out. Much of what I took out on Kenny, in the beginning, he did not deserve. But praise God for a man so patient, loyal, willing, and strong. I am so grateful that he did not leave because of the unhealed, broken, emotional parts of me that I didn't know how to control or didn't allow to heal. He knew that pain and brokenness I felt because he too was in an unhealthy marriage years before that as well. I truly believe we just learned to intentionally appreciate one another because we were tired of the pain and unhealthy relationships. But, we also knew that healing would be a journey for me and it wouldn't happen overnight.

After a few months, Kenny decided it would be best if he moved back with his mom. After a few days of thinking if that would be best for him he decided that it would be, so he could get his finances in order. I wasn't sure what this would look like for us all since I had already begun to stay with him at his apartment, although not fully moved in. Kenny, I, and the kids all moved into his mother's townhouse, and I was so grateful that she took us in. It was tight, but we made it work out the best way we knew how being that it was only temporary. We stayed in a small bedroom big enough to fit a twin-size bed, a dresser a playpen, a desk, computer, and TV for Kenny to be able to work and that's about it. We barely had room to walk around in, but we didn't complain.

Talk about humble beginnings. At this time Kenny and I shared a car, and we made it work. The kids were going back and forth to their dads' house every other weekend and while they were with us they slept on the couch at Kenny's mom's house. It was really a time for us all to get used to and try hard to be grateful for all we did have and not complain about what we didn't have.

We knew of the Lord and at one point had served Christ but had fallen away. We tried visiting a church that I attended before leaving but it just didn't feel right for us. So, we kept searching. We heard a church was opening up close by, and we decided to visit. We began visiting High Place Church in 2014 and never stepped foot in another church again. It was so freeing to be there. We felt the presence of the Lord in that place, and genuine love from the pastors and elders and it felt like home. We knew we belonged there.

Kenny wasn't as invested as I was once we began attending. He would only go on Sundays and opted out of going Wednesdays because he thought it was a lot going more than once a week. I would go alone but continued to pray that the Lord would change his heart because I knew me forcing him wasn't the best thing to do. I learned to never stop praying no matter how long it took. I wanted him to love the Lord and attend because he wanted to, not because I wanted him to go. Not much time went by when he started telling me he actually wanted to go with me on Wednesdays and I knew it was the Lord working and that my prayers weren't falling to the ground. I was excited because we needed God to be our foundation.

I experienced Kenny get saved, we became members together, he was baptized, he began to serve, we started tithing, he would worship; hands lifted high,

I've witnessed him get filled with the Holy Spirit and so much more. It has been such a beautiful, priceless journey to watch my husband's relationship with the Lord flourish. We both have grown so much in our home church, and we couldn't be any more grateful.

The closer we got to God and the more we listened to the word our pastor preached from the pulpit, the more we began to know that we needed to surrender every part of us to God. That being said, we began feeling a strong conviction about us living together and sleeping together. We decided that we would stop being intimate with one another because we wanted to please God and wanted him to bless our relationship. Imagine how that went. We failed so many times. Every time we failed, we would feel terrible, I would cry out of shame, and he would feel bad seeing me cry.

Many times we would stop in the middle of it because we felt a strong conviction, it was tough. Sex was created by God to be pleasurable in marriage. (*Hebrews 13:4*) We weren't married and I knew that if we continued to do it we would be living in sin, and we wanted to surrender everything, not pick and choose what we wanted to surrender and not surrender. I knew living with him and trying to stop being intimate was hard. So, I asked my mom if I could move back in with them because I wanted to do right by God's word. She declined and said that she was trying to get rid of those who lived there temporarily out of her house. I cried. I cried a lot because, as much as I understood my mother's point, I was trying to do right by God's word and live as He asked us to, but I guess that mattered more to us than anyone else. It was definitely a season where self-control for us was being tested majorly. We failed and kept failing, but there came a point where we were tired of feeling horribly convicted, and we did it. WE STOPPED. We stopped being intimate. I can attest that it was one of THE HARDEST things we had to do in that season or in general at that.

In the last few days of December 2015, we were approved for our very first brand-new apartment together. We were very happy and felt blessed that we finally had our own space. We loved the little apartment that was perfect for us in that season, minus our loud, obnoxious, rude neighbors we had above us and below us, but that's another story. We enjoyed the fact that our kids had their own space, we didn't have to feel so overcrowded. The kids had their own rooms and their own bathroom, and we all had plenty of space to feel a bit of freedom when we drove each other crazy. It was great and we were pleased.

February 7, 2016, to be exact, was also Superbowl Sunday that year. We had Sunday church service and the Pastor preached a sermon and one thing he said during that sermon was something along the lines of, "Men, if you have someone that you know you have been wanting to marry and been wanting to propose to, you better put a ring on it." Well, that day we had a house-warming party/Superbowl party at our apartment that we had moved into a couple of months prior.

Kenny stepped out with my brother and told me he had to go grab something. I thought it was something for our party, so I just said, "okay." As the evening grew older, and we were gathered in the living room because we were opening our house-warming gifts, it happened! Kenny yelled to everyone to be quiet and listen up. He got down on one knee and continued by telling me how this thing with us happened out of nowhere and that we have grown so much together in the two years we had been together. He told me he wanted to continue doing this, that he loves me and that he wanted to marry me.

He asked, "Would you marry me?"All of our friends and family watched, yelled, and screamed as I said, "Of course." And...... he PUT A RING ON IT!!!!!!!!!!!!! My goodness, if that wasn't one of the sweetest, most genuine moments of my life, I don't know what is. I was on cloud nine. No, it wasn't the most expensive ring in the world, probably a little over one hundred dollars, because we aren't rich, but that did not matter to me at all and still doesn't. The ring was beautiful and today, I still admire my ring, the proposal was even more beautiful, and I was blessed to be able to share that moment with him and those present.

What matters most is how he loves me, how he is present, and how consistent and faithful he has been.

Later that year we were married, after the required premarital sessions with our pastors. We had the best wedding ever. Many people say their wedding was a blur because of how stressed out they were at the wedding. I could honestly say we had an amazing, blessed, unforgettable day. Our entire day was dedicated to the Lord. We didn't get the fanciest ballroom, the biggest wedding cake, the most expensive rings, we didn't invite everybody and their momma just to feel important.

We had the best guests, those that meant the most to us in that season. We enjoyed it to the fullest, we remember every part of our wedding, and we would do it all over again the same exact way if we could. We wrote our own personal vows, made up our own personal handshake after we said, "I do," and it was probably the only wedding in history where the pastor married a couple sitting down because my pastor hurt his leg a few weeks before that, and we didn't want it any other way than having him marry us for our special day. Although we have never experienced a honeymoon after our wedding we are able to say that God has blessed us in our marriage and has shown us grace and mercy then and now. My husband is a great example of how Christ loves The Church. He wakes up early and dedicates his mornings to digging deep into God's word and he makes me yearn to draw closer to God

Here's what I learned:

Being Patient with what God has for you is far better than rushing into what may taste or feel good for a moment. It's like ordering fast food that will satisfy your stomach but not your overall health. Prepared and Cooked food, is far better than a fast unhealthy meal.

Ask yourself, have you been too impatient with God?

I will want you to understand that being patient does not mean we don't work at what God has for us. Remember we must:

1. **Prepare** - John C. Maxwell Once said - Seek the understanding, before seeking to be understood.

2. **Cook** - Create value in your relationships, whether that's marriage, business, or family.

3. Serve - Give willingly and with intention, never for self-gain. The reward is so much sweeter in the end.

CHAPTER ELEVEN

HEALED FROM THE INSIDE, OUT

Three months after we said, "yes" in committing to one another and God in marriage we found out that we were expecting our fourth child. We were ecstatic because our hearts were set on getting pregnant shortly after we were married if that was God's will. I remember taking multiple pregnancy tests just because we were excited to get pregnant. Many of them were false and it was a bit frustrating especially to someone like me, well, because I can be very impatient. But that moment we received a positive, we were extremely joyful. I remember laying the pregnancy test on the bed and my husband walking in the room and seeing it. The look on his face was a look of pure joy and many emotions running through his body.

About three months into the pregnancy our obstetrics (OB) doctor asked if we would like them to perform an ultrasound to determine genetic abnormalities if any. We agreed, but only because we were so excited to see our baby and this was the chance to be able to do so this early. It had nothing to do with learning about any genetic abnormalities because that was our least concern. I never agreed to have this testing done with any of my other pregnancies in the past, as I have always declined. The ultrasound was alarming to the doctors, so they sent me to get blood work. I did, and those results determined that I was at a 76% chance that our child would be born with trisomy 21, also known as Down Syndrome. The way I felt at that moment could never be explained well enough for anyone to be able to understand unless you have been in my position before.

I felt such pain and confusion because the doctors gave the news to us as if it were one of the most horrific things for a parent to have to endure. My husband and I were familiar with the term down syndrome before, but we never knew exactly what down syndrome was. Growing up, I would see individuals who had down syndrome and my heart would smile. I would think that they were the cutest, and most loving individuals anyone could come across. My mind began having flashbacks. Could it be that God gave me the heart to love and admire those individuals as a young kid, long before I ever knew I would even carry and steward over a child with down syndrome myself?

After all, He knows our life's journey way before we even live it. I don't recall anything more at that particular doctor's appointment aside from them sticking us into a room with a counselor who assists families who receive a diagnosis such as ours. They asked if we had any questions or concerns at the moment. But, the only question I had at the moment was, "how?" "How could this have happened", and, "how could this have happened to US?" Of course, the only reply I received to answer those questions was, "that we did nothing wrong to receive this diagnosis." I was still confused because I was ignorant. I was ignorant of the term Down Syndrome, let alone Trisomy 21.

The counselor explained that the average individual carries 46 chromosomes in their DNA but, individuals with Trisomy 21, carry 47 chromosomes and the third copy is found in the 21st chromosome. This is why we celebrate March 21st (3/21).

My husband and I were overwhelmed with this news and many thoughts running through our minds about the unknown.

The unknown is a scary place to be. We met with our spiritual leaders which are our pastors, I cried ... a lot, and explained to them all that we learned about our pregnancy thus far. They talked with us and prayed with us, but for some reason, my mind was still very uneasy. Our pastors were continuously reassuring and encouraging us that no matter what the outcome would be, to remember that God is in control and His will is far greater than ours. I had known that, but I was also allowing my emotions and fear to get the best of me because I didn't know what to expect.

I had never been a parent of a special needs child before. Many thoughts filled my head. Would I be adequate for this role? Was does this consist of? Will our lives change for the better? For the worse? I wanted to try to have it all figured out, yet I didn't even have a confirmed diagnosis. I wasn't able to fully enjoy my pregnancy because practically every doctor's visit, they would suggest that we abort our child. We frequently had ultrasounds done. Like, really intense, in-depth ultrasounds where they check every part of the baby's body very intently.

At one of the doctor's visits, they told us that the baby would have major heart issues and brain issues and that he would come out pretty much like a "vegetable." They told us it would probably be best that we abort because the complications would be too extreme. I was angry, furious, hurt, confused, all those emotions you could imagine, I felt. I left almost every doctor's appointment in tears. How could this be happening to us? After all, we had already been through in previous relationships, in life in general, why couldn't we just be able to enjoy our pregnancy without feeling like we had to hear these painful words. My husband was very supportive through it all.

He is naturally a very easy-going individual that doesn't let much of anything bother him, but that didn't mean he didn't have any emotion towards what we were going through because he did, he just handled it differently than I did. I had gotten to the point where I had to go to the doctor's office and almost block them out because I didn't want to hear the negative news about my son. My husband and I agreed that we would listen, but not actually accept what they were saying to us because we did not agree with aborting no matter how bad they said it would be.

We had to have more faith and not fear. We didn't want to abort just because they said that I should. We arrived at another doctor's appointment and my husband and I had a very serious and stern talk with our doctors and told them we don't care what any of these ultrasounds and test results say, we refuse to abort our son and would gladly appreciate if you would stop suggesting that we abort our son.

We are believing in a healthy son and are accepting him as he is. I remember having a discussion with my pastor and due to my ignorance of knowing nothing at all about down syndrome and fear of the unknown I asked, "Do you believe if our son was born with down syndrome God could heal him?" I would pray and my prayer went something like this, "Lord, please help and change this diagnosis, please heal my son Lord. I don't think I can do this God, I don't think I am built for this Lord. I'm scared, please help me, God." Not knowing all along that my prayers were ignorant and my prayers were trying to manipulate God's hand to do what I wanted, rather than what He wanted, which was His perfect will for my life.

The prayer I shared and was transparent about is real and I'm not sugar-coating that I allowed my flesh, ignorance, selfishness, and feelings to get in my head. I'm not going to paint a picture to my audience and make it seem like I was ecstatic to hear this news knowing that I was completely hopeless and hurting on the inside. Not to mention we went through this all alone because we didn't share this news with anyone, except our pastors, That's it! We needed prayers warriors, not pitied worriers and sometimes fewer people in your ear is the best wisdom you could use. *#prayersoverpity*

The day came when I delivered Kristian. After a very long thirty-five plus hours in labor after being induced our bundle of joy was here. I was so excited to see him and hold him, but I didn't get the opportunity to. As soon as he was born they put him in the baby cart and began to roll him away to the NICU. I never had any of my children pulled away from me as soon as I delivered them. I asked if I could take a picture of him before they took him. They stopped, I snapped two shots of Kristian and they rolled him away and we weren't able to see him for hours.

I was sad, all I wanted to do was hold my baby. I was in the room with my husband and my mother at the time. My mom didn't know anything about the possibility of him having down syndrome, so I texted my husband asking him if he felt that Kristian had down syndrome. He said, "no". I told him that I actually did feel he had down syndrome because I noticed his beautiful almond-shaped eyes which are a characteristic of individuals with down syndrome, but we just sat and waited with anticipation to see our boy. After some time went by the doctor came in and confirmed that he did in fact have Trisomy 21. My mom looked at me extremely confused and asked what that was because she wasn't familiar with what the term meant. I explained to her what it meant and she was very supportive and encouraged me that everything would be okay and he will be loved by our family no matter what.

The doctor continued to tell us that how they determined he had Trisomy 21 was that he had a straight line across his palm, if someone without Trisomy 21 whose line in their palm is curvier, she said he had "sandal toes", which means his big toe and the toe after were spaced a bit apart. She also mentioned that he had torticollis, which is weakened muscles and his ears were a little lower on his head. So, when Kristian would sit up his head would tilt only to one side until he was given physical therapy which started at about 4 weeks old, and that helped him tremendously.

The doctor asked us if we had any concerns or questions and was very supportive of us. She asked what our biggest concern was, and mine was that the older he got I would be afraid of bullies, and kids that would make fun of Kristian for seeing him as different. Truth is, we all are different special needs or not, we have all been created uniquely in God's eyes.

The time came when they finally allowed us to see our baby boy and hold him. I adored him the moment I saw him. He had complications due to breathing issues, he couldn't hold his own body temperature, and he had blood-related issues so he had to stay in the NICU for ten days after birth.

Any time we wanted to see him we had to scrub down in a very large sink, we couldn't have visitors, we had to wear yellow gowns, and were only able to visit. He had to stay in the NICU without us. When I was discharged I felt empty, I felt a void and I cried every day at the hospital. As much as we were able to we would visit Kristian.

I hated when it was time to leave I cried the entire drive home. Having to leave my baby was very hard and I cherished every moment there. I couldn't wait until he was able to come home because in those moments all I wanted was to have my family under one roof and to allow my kids to meet their baby brother. He was discharged once he was able to down a certain amount of milk. Once he could sustain his own body temperature when he could breathe on his own without an oxygen machine. And when his platelet numbers were high enough. It was a journey having to make sure his platelets stayed at a safe number. Platelets are the red blood cells that clot your blood when you get a cut to make sure you don't bleed too much where it can be life-threatening.

It was exhausting having to go to the doctor's office 2-3 times a week for blood. But we sacrificed to make sure he was okay. He had one of the best hematologists ever. She was on top of all of Kristian's labwork. Early on he had a genetic test was done which showed that at some point in his life he could potentially develop leukemia, even as old as an adult. There was no accurate time frame in knowing when or even if he would ever get leukemia. That terrified me knowing that and we prayed hard for God to always cover our son and protect him, but He had other plans and His ways are always higher than our ways.

When we first brought Kristian home from the hospital he had to see child development and cardiologists often and started Early Intervention at about 4 weeks old as I mentioned earlier. He was eventually able to sit up straight without a tilted neck, they helped him strengthen the muscles in his legs, arms, neck, and, feet, they helped with speech and as he grew older even had an occupational therapist and a teacher come out to help with play-time, puzzles, sounds, begin teaching him to feed himself and so much more. It was a long three years of having these therapists visit our home and work with Kristian a few times a week, but I'm so grateful for the assistance in helping Kristian get where he is now.

When Kristian turned one he had a fever that came out of nowhere. We took him to the ER and they were unsure where it was coming from also. We also learned that while he was there he had pneumonia but no symptoms of pneumonia were detected. They treated him for pneumonia and sent us home. A few weeks after that he developed another fever, again we took him to the ER again. At that point, the doctors were concerned and had him transported to DuPont Children's hospital in Delaware where we spent one night so they could evaluate and keep an eye on him. They discharged Kristian the next day but told us to keep a close eye on him.

His hematologist put in another set of labs and she told us she would call us with the results. We waited with anticipation in our dance studio that we owned at the time. While we were there I told my husband that I was very worried and that I hoped that God knew I couldn't handle my son having cancer and that I prayed we received good, positive results when his doctor called. My husband reassured me that all would be well and that God was taking care of things behind the scenes, all we have to do is TRUST HIM. Looking back I realized that God already knows what we can handle and what we can endure even if we feel that we can't, He knows we can because He strengthens us to do so.

The end of the doctor's shift was almost done and she stayed a little longer to be able to give us results before her shift ended. She called us and said that his tests seemed abnormal and she would like us to go to CHOP in Philadelphia to get a second opinion. We called the insurance company which told us that CHOP did not take the insurance we had at the time. I called our hematologist and told her that, she was not very happy she and I had to put in a claim to the insurance company to fight for Kristian to get at least one approved visit to CHOP. After a few long days of waiting, we finally received approval for one visit.

On June 19, 2018, our other three kids' last day of school and we had plans to take them out for finishing their school year strong. We had plans to visit CHOP first and then proceed to our family outing. But what happened that day changed our lives forever. We sat in the hospital for hours. They examined Kristian, did blood work, and hours later came back saying that they did a microscopic view of Kristian's blood cells and it was determined that Kristian did in fact have AMKL leukemia. I couldn't believe what I was hearing. My 17-pound little boy was diagnosed at just 14 months old. I was sick to my stomach, I wanted to crawl under a rock and never come out. However, I knew I couldn't because I had four children looking at how I would respond to this terrifying news. They told us we would not be going home because they needed to begin chemotherapy treatment on Kristian right away and also do a bone marrow sample and that he would be admitted right away.

There was no time for me to get into my feelings at that moment as hard as it was not to burst into tears. The first things I began to think about were finding who would care for our other three children, then moving into how long our son's treatments would be. What would all of this look like? We had no time. No time to plan for this. No time to cry. No time to be angry. We had to MOVE!

First, we huddled in a circle in the hospital room as a family and prayed around Kristian. Then, we called our pastors, mentors, parents, and sisters who were all very supportive and began praying for us. THIS.

WAS. HARD. Harder than hearing that our son would have Down Syndrome. We didn't know what this cancer could do to our son's little body. They told us if we did not start chemo right away he potentially would not survive. After we made arrangements for our children with my parents to care for them we were admitted and went through what the doctor's called a "Road Map" of his treatments. Which were just an outline of what his treatments would look like and an estimated time frame. They told us that he would need about 3-4 cycles of treatment and that it would be about a total of about 300 days.

They began his treatment right away. The first bag of chemo began being pumped into his body and all I could do was lie on the hospital bench in our room and cry. I felt numb. I was sick to my stomach. I felt like it all was finally hitting me. It was so hard laying in that room watching my youngest son being pumped chemo and me not being able to do anything in the natural realm, but one thing's for sure, I knew I could pray! It was my moment where I sensed God saying, "you say you trust Me, well show me that you trust Me." It was a moment where I had to really begin asking myself if I really did trust God or was it something that I just said because it sounded good.

This moment was the moment where I truly had to trust God, I had no choice. I was a desperate mother in need of God to heal and save my son.

The doctors told us he would most likely regress on his progression for his physical therapy. Kristian was barely sitting up before he was admitted to the hospital and we thought it would be a while longer before we witnessed our son sit up, stand up, crawl, etc. Within, three days he began sitting up in his hospital bed. Within a few weeks, he began pulling up on the crib he was in. The nurse had to lower his mattress because we were afraid he would fall out because he was showing so much strength during the first cycle. It was amazing to see God's power working in that short time already. The nurses told us he would probably vomit and, not want to eat or drink due to the chemo making him nauseous. Again, he ate every meal he had during his stay, and he didn't vomit, and we aren't sure if he was ever nauseous because he didn't talk and he was given medication just in case, but to our knowledge, we don't believe he was. God was STILL faithful and He had everything under control.

Kristian was so strong throughout every cycle he had to go through in there. He endured many needle sticks, bone marrow samples to be tested, blood transfusions, platelet transfusions, chemotherapy through IV and by mouth, nausea medication, and so much more. He inspired me so much as his mommy because I couldn't believe how strong he was, how much he was progressing and how happy and pleasant he was through it all. Bed baths became normal for us because he had a broviac in his chest, which was a needle that went into his chest to the vein in his heart that pumped the chemotherapy in.

Between each cycle, we were able to go home for about two weeks before starting a new cycle. The doctors told us that his first cycle would be the longest and that it would be about 32 days. They were right because after his chemo his immune system was totally wiped out, which meant he had to be confined to the hospital room and we had to limit visitors because he could easily catch an infection with no immune system. His immune system was 0 for about 12 days straight which was the longest 12 days ever for us. Waking up each morning wondering if the daily 4 am blood draws showed that his immune system was back to normal. Every morning that we heard that they weren't I wanted to scream! But eventually, he was allowed to go home after 32 days of being there. After his first cycle, he was in remission. Praise God.

While we went home on breaks in between cycles we were able to spend time with our three other kids at home which was nice. Otherwise, they would visit us in the hospital and could come daily to spend time with us. It was challenging because we have never been away from our kids that long. We had to make sure we were still spending time with them and acknowledging their feelings about everything happening and including them was important.

For me, being in one room took a toll on my mental health. Being confined to one room for 32 days was HARD. I felt like that hospital room became my prison cell. With time I began sensing that that time for me was my "cave season." The season where God wanted to have me to himself and work some things in and through me. The time when He had to prick away at some things and some people.

During treatment, my husband would begin dancing with Kristian while in the hospital. Every couple of days Kenny would dance to keep Kristian's spirits lifted. I have never seen something more precious than my son and my husband having this amazing bond with each other.

It was so awesome that we just had to record it for our keepsake. My husband often times spoke about keeping a positive atmosphere in the room and outside of the room. So we decided to post their dance videos online to our friends and family.

And with every post, Kenny and Kristian were putting smiles on people's faces from all over the world. The videos got so much attention that even stars like Ciara, Steve Harvey, Janet Jackson, and more got wind of it and supported our family with their gifts, prayers, and love.

Kenny saw what God was doing in our lives, even in the middle of a horrible storm, God used our family to be the encouragement to many that were fighting a storm that they felt they couldn't get out of. Which each video a story was told and lives were inspired.

You never know how God will use you. I'm so thankful for my husband for remaining obedient during that time. And even remaining strong when I felt I could not. Sometimes we have to lean on someone else strength along the journey and that's ok. Just as long as you never quit even if you feel like it. The big lesson here is to always remain faithful and obedient. You never know who you will bless with your mess.

He needed silence from us. He wanted me to trust Him and Him alone. He showed me those who needed to be in my life for that season, and those who didn't belong in that season. It was rough. A season of pruning and stripping away. A season of loneliness. A season of trusting Him. A season of being at His feet, silent and listening. I had to change my perspective of why I was there. It's easy to ask God, "why me." But, why not me? We made sure that even throughout Kristian's treatments we would stay committed to attending church to make sure spiritually we were being fed. We had Kenny's mom and one of my friends rotate in watching him Sundays and Wednesday's so that we could still attend church, which was important for us.

During his third cycle we asked the doctor if he could order a chest X-ray for Kristian because something didn't seem right with Kristian, and being that we are the parents we know our child best, so I would never step back from a doctor saying my child seems to be okay when my gut is telling me otherwise. He declined the X-ray and I was livid. We went back and forth with the doctor for a few minutes on reasons why we felt he needed an X-ray. We were trying to rule out pneumonia because Kristian had it in the past, but he had no symptoms of pneumonia. The doctor was the head doctor of oncology yet denied our son an X-ray and walked out of the room. My husband saw how upset and angry I was, to the point of tears because I wanted to flip out. So, he followed the doctor down the hall and had a man-to-man conversation with him. He finally put in an order for an X-ray for Kristian. We spoke to the manager of the nurse's department and told her that we wanted that doctor on Kristian's team removed, and he was. We were not dealing with anyone that was that rude and ignorant of our needs for Kristian we didn't care what title they had at the end of their name. Thankfully, we were persistent about that X-ray because it did not show pneumonia but what it did show was even worse. It showed that Kristian's broviac was pulling out from his chest and if it wasn't caught when it was he could have had a major infection that could have been life-threatening.

Parents, you know your child the best. Don't ignore your motherly/fatherly instincts in letting others even doctors and nurses tell you any different. Better to be safe than sorry.

During one of Kristian's final cycles, we had a few different times when things became scary for him. I was woken up one morning at 3 am by the large over-the-bed hospital spotlight and doctors flooded our room. Imagine waking up to that. I was thinking the worst and asked what was going on. Kristian's broviac had two tubes hanging from it. One for the chemo, and one for his medications aside from the chemo. Well, one of those tubes had a hole in it and the chemo stopped flowing through it. It could have burst which would not be good. I was nervous because I wasn't sure what was going to happen, how would they solve this?

They ended up being able to cut where there was a tiny hole and replace the tube with another tube. The way they were yanking at his broviac looked painful and I was not happy. It was red and began to get a bump around it from tugging so hard at it. After about an hour they were done and we thought that would be it. A couple of days later I had woken up again to the same exact situation, except it was the other tube. They ended up doing the same thing to the other side. We needed it to last just a few more weeks until his last treatment. Thankfully, after both of these replacements, it lasted until the end.

We were nearing the end of his cycle. We were in the 4th cycle. We had one more cycle left to go before he was released for good. My husband was running errands and one of his doctors came into the room and began to share that they needed to add one more cycle of high-dose chemotherapy before his final cycle. I was confused and instantly felt a dark cloud come over me. Something did not sit well with me and instantly felt my knees shake and I wanted to fall to the ground. I was not okay and asked her where this was all coming from because that is not the plan that was made in the beginning. She said, "children with down syndrome and this type of leukemia were dying more recently and to be safe they needed to do another high dose of chemo." I had questions. Why wasn't the high dose given in the first cycle? How "high" is this high dose? Why wasn't this talked about when he was first diagnosed? Why now? She didn't have all the answers to my questions so said she would meet with me later that evening.

The moment she walked out I called my husband crying hysterically. Instantly, I felt in my gut to decline that high-dose round of chemo. My husband also was not in agreement with it but we wanted to speak with our pastors before making a decision. So, we did. We contacted our pastors so they could pray and fast alongside us on what we should do concerning this matter. That evening the doctor came in to speak with us and stated that she didn't have all the answers to my questions but what she did know was the chemo dosage was 15 times more than the chemo he was already getting, two minutes later she corrected herself and stated, "oh no, I mean it will be 30 times more than the chemo he was receiving." So many red flags and the answers just continued to not sit well with us. She said that they used to give this high dose but stopped and since kids were dying more recently they decided to start it up again. Everything about this was just not okay with us. There were times I had questions that she had to google the answers to as I stood there and watched her.

I reached out to a couple of doctors in different states to get their opinions about it and a couple of parents with a child that had the same diagnosis as Kristian. After much thought, prayer, fasting, and advice we decided to go with what the Spirit was saying. One evening as I knelt on the dirty hospital bathroom floor in tears, I asked, "Lord please lead me in which way to go so we don't make a decision we could potentially regret." We were feeling like what if we made the wrong decision concerning our son's health? That would be something we would have to live with. That was very hard for us. We went back and forth for days. As I cried out to the Lord on the hospital floor I heard Him say, "stick with the roadmap." Then this played in my mind, "if you were traveling with a paper map like the old days before GPS existed, would you take any road to get to your destination? Would you go off-road? Most times not or you will get lost. Well, I sensed the Lord telling me, "stick with the road map. Stick with the roadmap, don't go off-road. The roadmap the doctors gave you did not say the sixth round of high-dose chemo. STICK WITH THE ROADMAP! So, that's what my husband and I decided to do and we felt confident about it.

When we explained to the doctor our decision she was not happy. My husband and I received a lot of hard feelings from the doctor. She said, "well if it was my daughter I would do it in a heartbeat." I said, "well listen, it's not your daughter or your son. Our decision we made came with lots of prayer and fasting and I would appreciate it if you respect that. She said if this was the beginning of Kristian's treatment and we declined anything like this they could potentially take us to court. I said, "well it's not the beginning we are more than halfway through, and we have been very on top of all his treatments for what was needed for him." She continued telling us that if we changed our minds we could bring him in after his last cycle.

Inside I was boiling because she just didn't want to take no for an answer. She kept trying to instill fear in me by telling me what could happen, and even what has happened to other kids. That is if it was even true. But we stood our ground and remained focused on what was told to us by Papa God. After Kristian was finished that round and we got to go home for a couple of weeks before his last cycle began, she called my husband's cell phone and again asked if we wanted to go with the high dose. She was so adamant about that last round. He told her, "with all due respect, we do not want to hear about another high-dose round. So stop bringing it up, and stop asking us about it, and let the other staff know not to bring it up to us again either." After that, we didn't hear about it anymore. It became exhausting hearing it over and over again and feeling pressured and somewhat bullied into doing something we didn't feel was best for our child. After all, all children are not the same. What works for one may not work for the other. That needs to be respected and understood.

After they hung his last bag of chemo on November 7, 2018, it felt like we were able to finally breathe and see some light at the end of the tunnel. He breezed through that last round. The doctors thought every cycle would be about 32 days or more and told us as the cycles get closer to ending he would be in the hospital for longer periods of time and that did not happen. God truly worked a miracle in our son and we had front-row seats to witness every bit of it.

The nurses, doctors, janitors, and any staff that walked into our room saw that there was light when they entered the room. They would sit in there and just conversate with us. They felt the love and peace in that room. They would share with us their personal stories about what they were currently facing. Here we are facing one of the most traumatic seasons in our lives yet, inspiring those we were coming in contact with. And for that, I give God all the Glory.

Our son has and still inspires millions across the world and for that, I am forever grateful to God for that. Thank You Lord for doing only what YOU can do.

As of June, 2022 Kristian is three years and 7 months cancer-free. Praise God!

CHAPTER TWELVE

BLOG ABOUT KRISTIAN

The amazing journey/testimony of our baby boy

Kristian Izaiah-Allen Thomas was diagnosed with Trisomy 21.

Every child-bearing mother's dream is that they birth to a child who is "perfect!" But what really is the definition of a perfect child?! In my eyes, the definition of "the perfect child" is the one Our God creates. Our God is perfect and He molded and shaped each and every one of us. Jeremiah 1:5 "I knew you before I formed you in your mother's womb. Before you were born I set you apart and appointed you as my prophet to the nations." This is scripture. You can't pick and choose what scriptures you believe and abide in. It says in his word that in the Lord, we are wonderfully made. My Kristian is fearfully and wonderfully made.

Being newly married my husband and I wanted to quickly have our very first child together, so shortly after marriage, we conceived. We were so excited! After a few doctor's appointments and, a few tests the doctors began telling us that we may be at high risk of having a child with trisomy 21. We were so confused and worried, that we left the doctor's office with alterations and felt so lost. All I could do was cry because they asked me to get further testing so I could be sure of the diagnosis in case I wanted to abort our innocent child if he did have trisomy 21. Trisomy 21, is another word for Down Syndrome which means our son has an extra 21st chromosome. How exciting and unique! But, I felt so furious! How could the doctors even be okay with telling a mother that? I later then realized that many women abort their children if they find out their baby has down syndrome. Personally, I could never do such a thing.

I declined the amniocentesis which is the test that supposedly determines if the baby definitely has the diagnosis or not. I told the doctors time after time I was going to keep my baby no matter what we do not care what the diagnosis is. We continued our prenatal care and just prayed every time w went to the doctors. Almost every visit the doctor stated that if I wanted the test I had to get it before a certain amount of weeks or I couldn't get it done, but I continued to decline. It seemed at almost every visit they would try to push me into finding out in case I wanted to abort, our son. In the room, I would rebuke the enemy and let their words go in one ear and out the other. I had to prepare myself before each visit but would break down once I got into the car. It hurt me so deeply because no matter what the outcome was we knew we were going to keep our son.

Don't get me wrong I was scared, nervous, anxious, confused and so much more, but I also wanted to enjoy my pregnancy. With the support of our Pastors and immediate family, we stayed as strong as possible and prayed up. One day Pastor Edgar was preaching a sermon and in his sermon, I remember clearly him saying," don't try and manipulate God with your prayers". That was a word I needed to hear because my prayers regarding my pregnancy because of my fear and ignorance were "God please no, don't let my son have Down Syndrome please God if he does please take it away."I cry as I write this because who am I to try and change what God has already created which is an amazing, perfect, beautiful, joyful baby boy. God checked me, I asked God for His forgiveness and my prayers began to sound more like," God whatever Your will is regarding Kristian let it be done, You know what we need, You know what we can handle and You know Your plans for our son.

I knew that if our son had Down Syndrome we would be so lost in what to do because we declined any and every help from the Doctors, but we knew God would be our help in everything and lead us along the way lacking-nothing. After a rough 36-hour labor, on April 11, 2017, I birthed an amazing child of God! Weighing 6 lbs 15 oz was our Little Pumpkin Kristian Izaiah-Allen Thomas. I anxiously waited to deliver so I could hold him, but also anxious to hear the news of his diagnosis. Due to some complications with Kristian during the delivery process and him being stressed, sadly I couldn't hold him. I literally got a 3-second glance at him in an incubator, took 2 pictures of him and he has pulled away from us and rushed to NICU.

I texted my husband because my mother was in the room and I didn't want to speak in front of her. I didn't want to worry her and I wasn't ready to face what the reality was not even to my family. I asked him if he thought the baby had the diagnosis because of his almond-shaped eyes, but he said, "no." I felt differently though but tried not to mention it again. Shortly after the doctor came into the delivery room and gave us the news. She said your baby definitely has Trisomy 21. My mother was very confused and all I could do was cry! I asked how do you know and she mentioned his beautiful almond-shaped eyes, the one crease that went across the palm of his hand, his ears that, are slightly lower than ours, and a few other things. I remember just crying and crying and crying.

My mother questioned what trisomy 21 was because she had never heard the term before. Just an FYI Down syndrome is NOT called Down syndrome because our kids are down, stupid, retarded, shameful, or any other ignorant terms people think are okay to say when they have no knowledge whatsoever. The title was created because the founder of the diagnosis's last name was Down, but he mentioned he hoped his last name was Awesome so he could title it "Awesome Syndrome" So we explained what it was to my mother and my family was very supportive hearing this which was very helpful.

Kristian spent 10 days in NICU due to a very low platelet count which is what helps your blood to clot, he was on an oxygen machine to help him breathe and had a feeding tube in to help him eat. That was emotionally stressful because you expect to deliver and take your baby home. When you can't it makes you feel so empty inside. We spent every day in the hospital with him as much as we possibly could including Easter day after church. I cried every time we would say our goodbyes each night because it hurt so bad to leave him. Our three other children were so upset because they couldn't meet him until we brought him home because he was isolated. Imagine the anticipation.

In the short 9, almost 10 months of Kristian's life, Kristian has seen hematologists (following him since birth), cardiologists, urologists, pulmonologists, occupational therapists, and physical therapists twice a week, and speech therapy monthly and has a teacher weekly. Soon seeing an audiologist and ophthalmologist. Right now he can't crawl, can't sit on his own completely, and has low muscle tone but is gaining strength. He's taking longer to grow his teeth. I know God got him through all the storms and tests. At the very beginning of this journey, I myself was so ignorant of the fact that I had a child with down syndrome because I was clueless about what to expect. (I am being very transparent just so the readers know how real it is and how real I am being.) I would think maybe it is a mistake, maybe they switched my baby after birth, but it's probably not true.

Imagine me going through this with someone God' didn't have destined for my life, it would be much harder. Don't question God, just be still. God knew He would give us Kristian after becoming husband and wife. Could you imagine me experiencing this with a "Bozo" rather than my "Boaz?" We are a team and with God, a three-fold cord could never be broken. I look back and I was just mixed with so many emotions and the fear of the many "what ifs" and how the doctors and nurses portray this all to be. It puts a major fear of the unknown in your mind. I know God chose my husband and me for a reason and I'm so glad He chose us! He chose us because He knew we could handle it, He chose us because He knew we would fight for our son, He chose us because

He knew we would do everything to make sure Kristian gets all the treatment he needs and the right way and He chose us because He knew if we didn't know what to do we would search for the answers. We were chosen because we look, to God for what plan He has for us and He gets all the glory, honor, and praise for everything He does in and for our lives.

As a young woman going into my 20s I had a heart for those with this diagnosis. When I would see a person with Down syndrome I didn't have to know them, but I felt so much joy and could sense that they are so loveable. I would think "oh my goodness I wanna hug them and squeeze them." What is it like to have a child that is always so loveable and happy? God was preparing my heart way back then. What do you do when God shocks you with HIS PLAN rather than your own? In Jeremiah 29:11 it says " For I know the plans I have for you says the Lord, plans for a hope and a future."God knows us better than we know ourselves, so His plans are always higher than ours. Our son has definitely changed our lives. He lets us see life from a different perspective. We are so busy with him and making sure he is always healthy and on track with everything. We just wanna make a difference for Kristian and those with a similar diagnosis.These kids are amazingly beautiful. He's special to us and we couldn't be more grateful to be his mommy and daddy! Our three other children are crazy about him and adore him. His first middle name Izaiah in Hebrew means "God is salvation."

Love always, Josilyne and Kenny Thomas & The Thomas Clan

Blog was written by Josilyne Thomas on 1/29/2018

CONCLUSION

I pray that you have enjoyed this book and all it had to offer. I know my life is far from perfect, but that is the reason why I had to share. Somewhere out in the world, there is someone going through some of these same experiences and thinking that they are at the end of their rope. But I want to encourage you. That you may feel like you are at the end of your rope, but you are never at the end of your hope. Keep The Most-High God First in your heart, and in everything you do. Stay firm on His perfect word and you too will be Restored. God bless!

Prayer

Lord, I thank You for giving us breath in our lungs daily. I thank You for allowing me to share my real-life story. I pray that anyone that may have read this book and can relate, that they feel Your love, Your grace, and Your forgiveness. I pray that those who are still bound by the things You intended for us to be free from, that they will call on You today. There is freedom in You Lord! Strip us from the feelings of thinking that we have to do things our way rather than Your way. Your will for our lives is perfect! I pray that You comfort those who are hurting in this season, who may feel unworthy of Your love, and who may be grappling with whether or not they should leave a situation that may be holding them back from Your calling. Give them the strength and the boldness to say YES to Your will and to Your way and no to the desires of the flesh. We love You and praise You for all that You're about to do. For You are The God of miracles. You are The God who sets free. And You are The God who breaks chains. Holy Spirit have Your way! In Jesus' name. Amen and Amen

Made in the USA
Middletown, DE
28 April 2023

29659262R00116